# CHRIST, THE CULMINATION OF THE LAW

## The Gospel for Religious Muslims

## Lessons from Jesus' Interaction with the Pharisees

## An Example in Reaching Religious Muslims with the Gospel

Bert de Ruiter

ISBN 978-3-95776-145-3



Photo credits (Cover):

Museum exhibits representing a Torah at the former Glockengasse Synagogue, which was in Cologne but was completely destroyed.
Author: HOWI (Horsch, Willy).
https://commons.wikimedia.org/wiki/File:K%C3%B6ln-Tora-und-Innen-ansicht-Synagoge-Glockengasse-040.JPG

Sermon on the Mount by Carl Bloch (1877).
https://commons.wikimedia.org/wiki/File:Bloch-SermonOnTheMount.jpg



VTR Publications, Gogolstr. 33, 90475 Nürnberg, Germany,
info@vtr-online.com, http://www.vtr-online.com.

# CONTENTS

# INTRODUCTION

*... the most important bridge Jesus offers between Christianity and Islam is his wisdom. The nature of Christ will continue to be a gap between the two faiths, but the teachings of Christ on faith, law and morals are binding. Muslims, in fact, desperately need that wisdom today, ... for they suffer from the exact same problem that Jesus saw at the Pharisees of his time: Obsessing about the minute details of religious law, while forgetting its moral purposes.*[1] (Mustafa Akyol)

This comment by Mustafa Akyol, a Turkish Islamic writer, confirmed something that I have been thinking about for quite a while. The Pharisees were an influential group of religious people, who sought to live according to the law of God and keep themselves pure from things that do not belong to the holiness of God. These are some of the similarities we can see between the Pharisees of Jesus' time and the religious Muslims of our day. More of these similarities are pointed out in this book.

Many Christians often assume that the Pharisees that Jesus had so many discussions and clashes with, were nothing more than religious hypocrites that constantly and consistently interfered with Jesus' ministry and who eventually were instrumental for His death. Also, many Christians have the impression that Jesus only condemned them and had nothing good to say about them. While it is true that when we read through the Gospels, we often read of Jesus condemning the Pharisees, this is not the whole picture that the Bible gives of them. We read about Pharisees who invited Jesus for a meal, and who warned Him about evil plans against Him. We also hear of Nicodemus, who came to Jesus with genuine questions. Jesus answered his questions, as we will see later in this book. We know of Saul, who met Jesus on his way to Damascus and who radically was transformed. Nevertheless, as we will see, even after his conversion Paul considered himself a Pharisee. Also, Paul's spiritual teacher, Gamaliel did prevent the Jewish Sanhedrin from killing the apostles. Might he be a man of peace, a concept that is regularly referred to in modern church planting?

---

1 https://www.huffingtonpost.com/entry/the-islamic-jesus-a-gap-or-bridge-between-christians_us_58dbc7dbe4b07f61a2bb8a55, (accessed March 18, 2021).

So, not everything that the Bible tell us about the Pharisees is bad. Jesus loved them and invited them to the eternal banquet in God's presence. We will see that He shared stories with them in which the truth of God was communicated to them.

Not only the Pharisees are looked upon negatively by many Christians, the same can be said about how, generally speaking, Evangelical Christians look upon Muslims. Their religion is seen as legalistic, their culture as backward, their religious commitments as evil and they themselves as unwanted. As a result, many Christians do not associate with Muslims and are reluctant to share their lives with them. But is this what Jesus wants? Jesus did spend time with the Pharisees, He did invite them to communion with God. As we will see Jesus socialized with them. He loved them and died for them. God, in His grace, compassion and love, reached out to the Pharisees and brought several of them to become followers of Jesus Christ.

In this book, I want to explore the similarities between the Pharisees of Jesus' day and the religious Muslims of our day. After discovering who the Pharisees were (chapter 1), we will look at four parallels between modern religious Muslims and the Pharisees (chapter 2). In chapter 3 we learn that Jesus' interaction with the Pharisees consists of confrontation, condemnation, and compassion. Chapter 4 discusses three of Jesus' lessons to the Pharisees that are applicable to religious Muslims of our day. Jesus' habit to relate to Pharisees can be summarized with the Arabic word for 'good habit': SAFT, as we will see in chapter 5. In chapters 6 to 9 we learn of several examples in the Bible of God at work among the Pharisees, which can be an inspiration and stimulate prayer and hope for God doing similar things in the lives of our Muslim friends.

As the conversation of Paul made clear, a conversion of a Pharisee is a conversion from the Law to Christ, because as we will see in chapter 10, Christ is the culmination of the law.

It is my desire that this book will encourage you to compassionately share your live with your Muslim friends and to provide you with some tools to do so. Tools that are taken from the way Jesus related to the Pharisees.

# CHAPTER 1
# WHO WERE THE PHARISEES OF JESUS' TIME?

*"The Pharisees ... are an intermediary group that bridges the gap between unbelieving Jews and believing Christians."*[2]

We know from the account of Jesus' life and ministry as written in the Gospels of Matthew, Mark, Luke and John that Jesus frequently was in contact with the Pharisees. The word 'Pharisee' occurs almost 100 times in the Gospels.[3]

**Who were they?**

The Pharisees were a religious, political, and social movement within Judaism. During the time of Jesus' ministry, the number of Pharisees is estimated to have been about six thousand.

The Pharisees were one of at least four major schools of thought within the Jewish religion around the first century AD.

The other groups were:[4]

*The Sadducees.* The Sadducees were conservative, wealthy, and aristocratic party of the status quo. They usually held the high priesthood and were the majority of the 71-member Sanhedrin Supreme Council. The Sadducees were prepared to work with Rome and Herods.

*The Scribes.* The Scribes were the copiers and interpreters of the Torah since before the exile. They were linked to the Pharisees, but some were also Sadducees and on the Sanhedrin Supreme Council.

*The Essenes.* The Essenes were a breakaway desert monastic group, especially at Qumran on the Dead Sea. They lived communally, without private

---

2 Gowler, David B. *Portraits of the Pharisees in Luke and Acts*, (New York: Peter Lang, 1991), 307.

3 29x in Matthew, 12x in Mark, 27x in Luke and 19x in John. There are 9 references in Acts and one in Philippians (3:5).

4 For more information about these and other groups, see https://catholic-resources.org/Bible/Jewish_Groups.htm.

property, as farmers or craftsmen under a Teacher of Righteousness and Council.

*The Zealots.* The Zealots were extremist fighters who regarded political freedom as a religious imperative. It was an underground resistance movement, especially strong in Galilee. The most fanatical became sicarii, dagger-wielding assassins.

## History of the Pharisees

Some consider Ezra, whom is spoken of in the Old Testament, the philosophical and religious forerunner of the Pharisees.[5] Ezra was a descendant of the high priest Aaron, and is described as 'a teacher well versed in the Law of God' (Ezra 7:6) and someone 'who had devoted himself to the study and observance of the Law of the Lord, and teaching its decrees and laws in Israel.' (Ezra 7:10)

During the time of exile there was the danger that the Jewish people would be absorbed into the gentile world. The Jewish people survived their religious identity during the exile mainly through one thing: the Law of God (Torah). Although the Torah, the Jewish law, had been the heart of the Jewish religion from the time of Moses, it became the centre of the community's life during the exilic period when Israel no longer had a temple at the centre of its life. As a result, the Jews in exile became 'a people of the Book' or of the Law. Through the devotion to the Law, Israel managed to retain its identity and from being assimilated by the foreign powers that dominated them.

In the period before the Maccabean revolt (167–161 BCE) there was a movement against increasing Hellenistic Jewish political leadership. This movement was known as the *Hasadim*. This movement felt that there was too much laxity among the people in keeping the law. The Hasadim emphasized a strict Torah observance.[6]

These Jews emphasized strict obedience to the law and observance of all Jewish customs, especially circumcision and Sabbath worship. All three of

---

5 Hovestol Tom, Extreme *Righteousness*, (Milton Keyes: Authentic Media Limited, 2013), 230.

6 Polhill, John, *Paul and His Letters* (Nashville: B&H Publishing Group, 1999), 28.

the major parties in first century Judaism (Pharisees, Sadducees and Essenes) developed from the Hasadim.

Among the Pharisees there were different sub-divisions, connected with the correct interpretation of the Law. Some documents refer to seven types of Pharisees.[7] Two schools became important: The House of Shammai (stricter) and the House of Hillel (gentler). These groups were in constant disagreement. Also, some Pharisees became attracted to apocalyptic speculation and the Zealots.

With the destruction of Jerusalem by the Romans in the year 70, the sect of the Pharisees died out and rabbinic Judaism evolved and continued developing the basic tenets of the Pharisees. Pharisaic Judaism became normative Judaism. Its principal features — the synagogue, the rabbi, prayer, Torah study, and belief in the oral law — became the modes of religious expression guiding Jewish life ever since. All Jewish life today, therefore, stems from the Pharisaic tradition and derives its central religious characteristics from it.[8]

## Lay teachers in the synagogue

After the Jews returned from exile, synagogues came into being. These were places of prayer and instruction in the Law.

---

7 Varner, William C. "Jesus and the Pharisees: A Jewish Perspective." *The Quarterly Journal*; The Newsletter Publication of Personal Freedom Outreach 16, no 3 (July–September 1996). Varner writes: "There is a passage, appearing in slightly different forms in both the Babylonian and Jerusalem Talmuds, that sheds an abundance of light on the self-perception of the Pharisees. This passage describes seven different types of Pharisees. A paraphrase of the difficult Talmudic language describes the following seven: (1) The 'shoulder' Pharisee wore his good deeds on his shoulder so everyone could see them. (2) The 'wait a little' Pharisee always found an excuse for putting off a good deed. (3) The 'bruised' Pharisee shut his eyes to avoid seeing a woman and knocked into walls, bruising himself. (4) The 'humpbacked' Pharisee always walked bent double, in false humility. (5) The 'ever reckoning' Pharisees was always counting up the numbers of his good deeds. (6) The 'fearful' Pharisee always quaked in fear of the wrath of God. (7) The 'Godloving' Pharisee was a copy of Abraham who lived in faith and charity."

8 Yehiel Eckstein, *What Christians Should Know About Jews and Judaism*. (Waco: Word Books, 1984), 258.

Pharisees were the lay religious teachers, who taught the law in the synagogues. While the Sadducees were more connected with the temple and its services, Pharisaism, mostly a lay movement, emphasized the importance of the study of its Scripture, especially the Law and its exact interpretation. Hence the Pharisees were above all the people of the synagogue, the 'house of study'.

> To the Pharisee the service of God was not primarily the sacrifice that took place in the Temple, but prayer and the explanation of Scripture. One could perform the synagogue service (which the Pharisees perfected) independently of the priesthood. To Pharisaism the whole nation was ideally called to be 'separated' so that to exalt one section into a priestly class was in effect to deny the essentially priestly character of the whole community.[9]

The service of God of the Pharisees consisted primarily in prayer and the explanation of Scripture, as opposed to sacrifice in the temple.

### Popular and influential

Although the Pharisees gradually became less involved in politics, they were very popular with the masses. Josephus writes that even though the Sadducees held all the major offices, they never made any important decisions without first consulting with the Pharisees.[10]

The Pharisees were popular among the common people and maintained leadership in spiritual matters.

> The Pharisees had the masses for their allies, the women being especially devoted to them. They held the greatest authority over the congregations, so that everything to do with worship, prayers, and sacrifice took place according to their instructions. Their popularity is said to have been so high that they were listened to even when they criticized the king or the high priest.[11]

---

9 Davies, W.D. *Introduction to Pharisaism*, (Minneapolis: Fortress Press, 1954), 14.

10 Quoted in Polhill, *Paul and His Letters*, (Nashville: B&H Publishing Group), 28.

11 Schürer, Emile, *The History of the Jewish People in the Age of Christ, Volume 2*; (Edinburgh: Bloomsbury Publishing PLC), 402.

> In the 1st century the Pharisees almost certainly formed the most influential section of the Jewish community. Their tenets in varying and modified degrees came to be accepted probably by the majority of the pious in Jewry.[12]

**Emphasized holiness and righteousness through the Law**

The Pharisees were committed to spend their whole life observing every detail of the Law of God. To them the Law was the most sacred thing in all the world. Religion, for the Pharisees, was unimaginable without the Law. They believed in it, and taught their followers to believe in as, as 'the Way, the Truth and the Life' as for them it really was.

They called on Jews to follow strictly the Law as they interpreted it.

> The Pharisees ... wished to embrace the whole people, and in particular through education. It was their desire and intention that everyone in Israel achieve holiness through the study of the Torah.[13]

Although in the mind of many modern Christians, Pharisees are synonymous for hypocrisy and legalistic religion, this probably was not the reputation they had in Jesus' time. They were known for their piety, holiness, and righteousness.[14]

Polhill points out that although "Pharisees are seen as wilful, prideful and self-righteous" this is not an accurate picture.

> They are depicted as attempting to pull themselves up by their own bootstraps to gain God's acceptance through their scrupulous observance of the law. Recent studies have emphasized that in most instances this is not an accurate picture of Pharisees. Most of them were well aware of their own sinfulness and dependence on God. Most tended to view the law as an expression of God's mercy, as a gift within his covenant relationship with his people. This is probably true.[15]

---

12 Davies, 17.

13 Bickerman, Elias. *The Maccabees,* (New York: Schocken Books, 1947) p 93.

14 Young, Brad H. *Jesus, the Jewish Theologian*, (Grand Rapids, Michigan: Baker Publishing Group, 1993), 184, 188.

15 Polhill, 29.

The Pharisees wanted to purify religion from empty rituals. They wanted to live a holy, righteous life. They strongly build their moral values upon the Law and Tradition.

> For the Pharisees, the Halachah was the definition of the will of God. The Halachah is the analogue of the Creed. For the Pharisees the doing of the divine will is the first and foremost essential of religion, whatever else might come after it.[16]

### Concentrated on purity

The word 'Pharisee' is derived from the Hebrew word 'Parush' meaning 'separated' or 'isolated', in the sense of being holy and sanctified, separated from the heathen. They emphasized separation in contrast to assimilation. They sought to strictly observe the Levitical purity and the avoidance of close association with anyone and anything impure.

They are sometimes described as a "body of Jews who profess to be more religious than others and to explain the laws more accurately."[17]

> Faced with social, political and cultural 'pollution' at the level of national life as a whole, one natural reaction ... was to concentrate on personal cleanness, to cleanse and purify an area over which one did have control as a compensation for the impossibility of cleansing or purifying an area – the outward and visible political one – over which one had none. ... The Pharisees tried to maintain purity at a degree higher than that prescribed in the Hebrew Bible for ordinary Jews under ordinary conditions ....[18]

### Interpreted the written Law through Traditions (oral law)

In their desire to apply the written Law of God in all possible aspects of life, they developed an oral law, based on the traditions of the elders. It was passed on by word of mouth from teacher to pupil. The oral law was not written down until AD 200, when the *Misnah* was published. In their desire to interpret the Law of God in all aspects of daily life, the Pharisees extracted

---

[16] Travers Herford, Robert. *The Pharisees*, (Basingstoke: MacMilland, 1924), 232.

[17] Finkel, Asher. *The Pharisees and the Teacher of Nazareth* (Leiden: Brill, 1964), 1.

[18] Wright, NT. *The New Testament and the People of God* (Minneapolis: Fortress Press, 1992), 189–195.

from the principles of the law an infinite number of rules and regulations to govern every conceivable situation in life. They did regulate their life by a Book, but even more by tradition.

They followed ancient traditions inspired by an obscure text in Deuteronomy, "put it in their mouths", that God had given Moses, in addition to the written Law, an Oral Law, by which learned elders could interpret and supplement the sacred commands. The practice of the Oral Law made it possible for the Mosaic code to be adapted to changing conditions and administered in a realistic manner.[19]

> The Oral Torah clarified obscure points in the written Torah, thus enabling the people to satisfy its requirements. If the Scriptures prohibit work on the Sabbath, one must interpret and define the meaning of work in order to fulfil the divine will.[20]

By accepting both the oral and the written Law, Pharisaism made possible the application of the Mosaic Law to everchanging conditions.

> The acceptance of tradition was the condition of adaptability. ... The essence of Pharisaism is the belief that religion (the gift and demand of God) covers the whole of life and that that religion is expressible in terms of Law. This meant that for the Pharisee it was possible by examination, exposition, and adaptation of the text of the Law to find what was the right conduct and to prescribe it for every circumstance in life. This seems to have been the Pharisaic ideal, the creation of a community governed by a code which provided a detailed chart which could be variously applied. They were the progressives ... who would make the Law of Moses a living reality, not an outward anachronism.[21]

### Several key theological beliefs

In comparison with other sects within Judaism, we find that several theological convictions of the Pharisees are similar to what Christians believe

---

19 Johnson, Paul. *A History of The Jews* (London: Weidenfeld & Nicolson, 1987), 106.

20 Young, 105.

21 Davies, 25.

such as: faith in afterlife, God's providence, God's justice and the coming Messiah. The Pharisees believed in the resurrection from the dead and the existence of spirit beings such as angels and demons. They balanced freedom and human responsibility. While they believed in divine providence, the election of Israel and predestination of many events, they also believed that humans have some freedom to make choices, but that God could and did interpose His will in men's lives. Josephus also wrote that the Pharisees believed "souls have an immortal vigour in them", and that men would be punished or rewarded in the next age based on how they conducted themselves in this life.[22]

Also, the Pharisees had messianic hopes; they were looking for the coming of the Messiah.

## Conclusion

We can identify the Pharisees as people who were devoted to the Law (of God) in order to retain their (religious) identity in a multi/anti-religious, pluriform and hostile world. They had a desire to conform to the revealed will of God as made known in the Law. They were deeply devoted to the knowing, interpreting, and applying the Torah to the daily life of the people of Israel in order to restore the fortunes of Israel.[23]

---

22 Josephus, The Antiquities of the Jews, Book XVIII, chapter 1, section 3, http://penelope.uchicago.edu/josephus/ant-18.html (accessed December 23, 2021).

23 Scott Mcknight, http://www.patheos.com/blogs/jesuscreed/2013/05/01/the-pharisees-my-response-to-the-new-barna-study/#ureYCqClb0Uekfj1.99.

# CHAPTER 2
# PARALLELS BETWEEN RELIGIOUS MUSLIMS AND PHARISEES

*"When I read the New Testament for the first time … I was struck by the passion, devotion, and sincerity I found in it. Particularly striking were Jesus' attitude to the Pharisees … Jesus was blaming these self-righteous pietists for their obsession with the minute details of the Halakha, while neglecting moral teachings that relate to the spirit. This sounded extremely similar to attitudes I see among some contemporary self-righteous Muslims pietists, who admonish fellow believers for not fully observing the minute details of the Shariah, or Islamic law, but neglect the moral teachings that relate to the spirit. Everything that Jesus said in Luke 11:42–46 … sounded very relevant to me and my own world of Muslim legalists."*[24]

Akyol is not the only one who sees parallels between the Pharisees of Jesus' time and modern-day Muslims. Missiologist Warrick Farah, writing a blog on 'Jesus, Pharisees and Muslims', writes: "Much of Islam parallels 1st century Phariseeism."[25]

In this chapter, I will focus on four parallels that I see between modern day religious Muslims and the Pharisees of Jesus time, namely:

- The emphasis on law and traditions.
- The emphasis on purity.
- A tendency towards legalism.
- A tendency to focus on external compliance.

## Emphasis on Law and Traditions

The Pharisees were devoted to the Law of God to retain their (religious) identity in a multi/anti-religious, pluriform and hostile world. The Pharisees

---

24 Akyol, Mustafa. *The Islamic Jesus: How the King of the Jews Became a Prophet of the Muslims,* (New York: St. Martins Press, 2017), 23, 24.

25 http://muslimministry.blogspot.nl/2009/06/jesus-pharisees-and-muslims.html, (accessed March 18, 2021).

had a desire to conform to the revealed will of God as made known in the Law and they build their moral values upon the Law of God. To them the Law was the most sacred thing in all the world. Religion, for the Pharisees, was unimaginable without the Law. They believed in it, and taught their followers to believe in as, as 'the Way, the Truth and the Life.'

For many religious Muslims it is important to live their lives in conformity to the will of God as found in the Sharia law. They seek to consume and behave in according to the Law of God (halal) and seek to stay away from consumption and behaviour that is prohibited by the Law of God (haram).

> Halal is a term designating any object or an action which is permissible to use or engage in, according to Islamic law. ... The opposite of halal is haram, which means unlawful or prohibited. Halal and haram are universal terms that apply to all facets of life. These terms are commonly used in relation to food products, meat products, cosmetics, personal care products, pharmaceuticals, food ingredients, and food contact materials ...[26]

Religious Muslims seek to live their lives in accordance with the Law of God as revealed in the Qur'an and like the Pharisees of Jesus' days seek to build their moral values and behaviour upon the Law of God. The reason for this is that the Law (Sharia) is considered to be a path leading to the spring, referring to God.

> ... the Sharia is the expression of individual and collective faithfulness, in time, for those who are trying in awareness to draw near to the ideal of the Source that is God. In other words, ... the Sharia shows us "how to be and remain Muslim." This means ... that the Sharia is not only the expression of the universal principles of Islam but the framework and the thinking that makes for their actualization in human history.[27]

The terms 'halal' and 'haram' are applied to all aspects of a Muslim's life and extends to include food, drink, clothing, behaviour, and practices. E.g. when

---

[26] According to the Islamic Council of Victoria (Australia) on their website. https://www.icv.org.au/about/about-islam-overview/what-is-halal-a-guide-for-non-muslims (accessed March 18, 2021).

[27] Ramadan, Tariq. *Western Muslims and the Future of Islam* (Oxford: Oxford University Press, 2005), 50.

it comes to food and drink there are a number of things which Muslims are not permitted to consume, such as alcohol or any other substance that may cause intoxication; the meat of pigs and any of its derivatives; the meat of any animal that has not been slaughtered according to Islamic Law; the meat of any animal that eats other animals and any of its derivatives. In terms of conduct in their daily lives, practices which are considered haram include: adultery; murder; gambling; earning interest; lying or cheating; backbiting or any other activities considered harmful to society at large.

We have seen elsewhere that that Pharisees of Jesus' time wanted to live a holy, righteous life. Their religious commitment was expressed in their commitment to the Torah, the Law of God.

Very similar sentiment can be seen among the religious Muslims of our day, who seek to obey the Sharia, the Law of God:

> The application of the sharia is considered a major manifestation of one's obedience to God which is deeply rooted in the conscience of the individuals and has a wide acceptance of the public in the Muslim society. It need not simply be the outcome of imposition by force. The position of the sharia in Muslim societies and the attitude of Muslims toward it is a main indicator of the depth of their religious commitment.[28]

Like the Pharisees considered the Law of God as the way to eternal life, many religious Muslims consider their obedience to the Law of God as their way to heaven. Although they seek obedience to Sharia, they understand that only God decides whether this has been enough to be allowed into paradise.

The Pharisees leaned heavily on the 'Traditions' in their desire to interpret the Law of God in daily life. This is like Muslims who lean heavily upon the Hadith and Sunnah (Traditions of Mohammed) for their interpretation of the Quran and their understanding of Sharia.

> The Qur'an is the message, while the Hadith is the verbal translation of the message into pragmatic terms, as exemplified by the Prophet. While the Qur'an is the metaphysical basis of the Sunnah, the Sunnah

---

[28] Karcic, Fikret. *The Other European Muslims: A Bosnian Experience* (Sarajevo: Center for Advanced Studies, 2015), 60.

> is the practical demonstration of the precepts laid down in the Qur'an ... Hadith, in practical terms, explains, clarifies, and paraphrases the Qur'an. If we reject the Hadith, we may misread the Qur'an; so Hadith is central to a proper understanding of the Qur'an ...[29]

## Emphasis on purity[30]

The Pharisees emphasized purity. We have seen that even their name 'Pharisee' is derived from the Hebrew word 'Parush', that means 'separated' or 'isolated', in the sense of being holy and sanctified. They sought to strictly observe the Levitical purity and the avoidance of close association with anyone and anything impure.

This emphasis on purity is also found among religious Muslims. Many religious Muslim consider ceremonial and moral purity as an essential element of their faith.

Ceremonial purity can be obtained by proper bodily purification e.g., making ablution, taking bath, cleaning teeth, using fragrance, keeping house and clothes clean etc.

For many Muslims, one of the most important aspects of prayer is that a person should be clean before performing them five times a day. This is in line with a Tradition that says that Muhammad said: *"The key to the prayer is cleanliness ..."* (Abu Dawud). Also, some Traditions indicate that prayers are said for the purification of the soul and for the cleansing of sins and mistakes.[31]

Before offering prayers, it is necessary for Muslims to perform *wudu*, which involves washing the hands, mouth, nostrils, arms, head, and feet with water. After sexual intercourse and menstruation, a full body wash (ghusl) is necessary. If the body or clothes show traces of urine, feces, semen, or

---

[29] Professor Shahul Hameed, former president of the Kerala Islamic Mission in Calicut, India, and a consultant for IslamOnline.net; https://archive.islamonline.net/?p=5322.

[30] http://www.quranreading.com/blog/importance-of-cleanliness-in-islam-quranic-verses-and-ahadith-on-purity/ (accessed March 18, 2021).

[31] (Muslim, Zikir, 73, Salat, 204), quoted in *A Comparative Dictionary of Religious Terms in Islam & Christianity,* M. Numan Malkoc and Peter Pikkert, (Ancaster: ALEV Books, 2020), 300.

alcohol, then purification becomes essential. In the Qur'an, these regulations are linked with God's desire to purify believers (Sura 5:5,6). Many juridical opinions add blood and pus to that list. The clothes should be washed, and the affected part of the body cleaned with pure water, or the whole body given a *ghusl* as the case may be. Someone who is not in a state of purity should not touch the Qur'an. Within Islam, purity is also related to food (i.e., what kind of food to eat and not eat) and people (whom to associate with). This emphasis on purity has resulted in what is considered permissible (halal) and what is not permissible (haram). Something is prohibited because it is considered impure.

Some Muslims point out that in Islam the physical and spiritual purity is integrated:

> Some Muslims emphasize that Islam doesn't view physical purity and spiritual purity as two different or apposing things because the equivalent of the English word *purity* in Arabic is *al-tahara*. The word tahara as used in the Quran is used in both the spiritual and physical sense (Sura 9:108; 2:222; 8:11).[32]

There are verses in the Qur'an that refer to moral purity. God wants to purify believers (Sura 3:141; 5:5,6; 33:33). God sent prophets to purify believers (Sura 3:164). Those who will be accepted in heaven are those that purify themselves, remember the name of their Lord and pray (Sura 87:14,15).

## Tendency toward legalism

The third similarity between many Pharisees of Jesus' day and many religious Muslims of our day is their tendency toward legalism.

Legalism has been defined as "the conviction that law-keeping is the ground for our acceptance with God — a failure to be amazed at grace."[33]

---

32 For example, Dr. Jamal Badawi, an Egyptian born Muslim Canadian and a well-known author, activist, preacher and speaker on Islam. http://jamalbadawi.org/index.php?option=com_content&view=article&id=50:52-pillars-of-islam-purity-a-hygiene&catid=17:volume-5-the-pillars-of-islam&Itemid=18 (accessed March 18, 2021).

33 John Piper in his talk "What is legalism?" https://www.desiringgod.org/interviews/what-is-legalism (accessed March 18, 2021).

> When you read their (Salafi-style Muslims BdR) books or magazines, you find everything they say about Islam is in terms of correct/incorrect (Such and such is not correct belief etc). It is admirable, of course, to be interested in the truth, but in their approach, there is no life, no love, no spirituality. It is all about legalism, such as the legalism of the Jews at the time of Prophet 'Esa. Hence, the recently coined condition of 'Salafee-Burn-Out' whereby people drop out of this movement after their heart has been completely drained of all spirituality.[34]

It is fair to say that what Emerick writes here cannot be applied to all religious Muslims, like it is probably an exaggeration to equate all Pharisees of Jesus' day with being rigorous legalists.

Nevertheless, both among Pharisees of Jesus´ day and among religious Muslims of our times, legalism plays a significant role. We find Jesus interacting frequently with the Pharisees addressing this issue.

Also, among modern day Muslims, legalism can easily become part of their religious life. In his book *Toward our Reformation: From Legalism to Value-Oriented Islamic Law and Jurisprudence*, Mohammad Omar Farooq advocates for a return to what he calls a "value-oriented" approach, to counter legalism.

> Legalism can be understood as a fixation on laws, codes of conduct, or legal ideas, without balancing with the mercy and grace of God. In the centuries since the time of the Prophet, Muslim societies tended towards legalism reducing everything down to black and white, right and wrong, or permissible and impermissible. Legalism makes people self-righteous while it induces in them a judgmental trait towards their fellow human beings. Legalism creates an environment where people are constantly worried about being improper, culminating in hair-splitting efforts over highly minute details of life. However, God does not intend that this world should be a place of perfection. More important is facilitating the human connection to and bonding with the Creator.[35]

---

[34] Yahya Emerick, writing about the Salafi-style Muslims. Emerick is former President of the Islamic Foundation of North America, vice-principal at an Islamic school, and a Muslim author; http://yahiyaemerick.blogspot.nl/2017/12 (accessed March 18, 2021).

[35] Farooq, Mohammad Omar. *Toward our Reformation: From Legalism to Value-Oriented Islamic Law and Jurisprudence,* "Chapter 2, Shari'ah, Law and the

Emerick suggests that Muslims of today need to learn from Jesus' approach:

> Muslims have lost touch, generally, with the noble qualities of Islam, qualities such as compassion, understanding, tolerance and progressiveness (from within an Islamic framework, of course). We have become like the Bani Isra'il: steeped in legalism, harshness and intolerance. In the same way that Prophet Jesus was sent to breathe new life into them, we must learn to reinvigorate ourselves.[36]

## Tendency towards external compliance

The last similarity between the Pharisees and religious Muslims that I want to highlight is their tendency toward external compliance. In fact, this is a trait that seems to be pervasive among all religious people, be it Christian, Jew, Muslim, or others. Unfortunately, religious piety can easily degenerate into external compliance only. While external compliance can be necessary and important, without heart compliance external compliance is hypocrisy and often closely connected to legalism, of which we have already spoken.

> Hypocrisy – especially the "religious" variety – stems from the assumption that living a "double" life is the best way to go. That is, have a public or external persona that people can respect, while reserving the right to host evil in your heart, and even enjoy the pleasures of sin when no one is looking. Of course, this religious hypocrisy, as Jesus states, is quite foolish, for it assumes that God thinks, acts, and sees like men do, and can be fooled by all this.[37]

In one of his discussions with the Pharisees Jesus referred to them as 'white graves' (Luke 11:44). He questioned their emphasis on outside purity, while being full of greed and wickedness on the inside (Luke 11:37–44). He warned others about the hypocrisy of the Pharisees (Luke 12:1). He referred to hypocrisy as 'leaven', referring to its permeating power of influence. Jesus also said that the words that Isaiah spoke of the religious people of his day, can also be applied to Pharisees: "These people come near to me with their

---

Qur'an: Legalism vs. Value-Orientation" (London: The International Institute of Islamic Thought, 2012).

36 Yahya Emerick, http://yahiyaemerick.blogspot.nl.

37 Dr. David W. Hegg in his blog: http://heggthought.blogspot.nl/2007/03/hypocrisy-and-legalism.html (accessed March 18, 2021).

mouth and honour me with their lips, but their hearts are far from me. Their worship of me is based on merely human rules they have been taught." (Isaiah 29:13; Matthew 15:7–9)

Of course, not all Pharisees were hypocrites, who were only interested in external compliance, but without a doubt many of them were or had a tendency towards being hypocritical, making religion something to be seen by others instead of a matter of the heart; a pursuit to please the public, instead of God.

Likewise, we cannot maintain that all Muslims are hypocrites that are only interested in outward performance without paying attention to serving God with the heart. Serving God with the heart and outward performance can go together. But when the outward and the inward do not line up, it can lead to hypocrisy. This kind of attitude is strongly condemned in the Qur'an: *"The hypocrites will be in the lowest depths of Hell, and you will find no one to help them."* (Sura 4:145)[38].

Regarding the Pharisees, Jesus spoke about their hypocrisy in financial giving, in praying and fasting. These are three of the five pillars, which shape the religious identity of Muslims and might explain why religious Muslims are susceptible to external compliance, particularly those coming from cultures where saving face is important.

There are some Islamic scholars who distinguish between two kinds of hypocrisy. *Major hypocrisy* and *minor hypocrisy*. Both are condemned, where the consequence of major hypocrisy is eternal hell, while those who are guilty of minor hypocrisy will be condemned to hell temporarily, while afterwards God might forgive him and provide him entrance into Paradise.

Major hypocrisy is the hypocrisy of one who conceals disbelief whilst making an outward show of being a Muslim.

> The one who pretends outwardly to believe in Allah, His Angels, His Books, His Messengers and the Last Day, whilst inwardly believing that which is contrary to that or part of it, is the hypocrite in the sense of major hypocrisy.[39]

---

38 "The Qur'an", translation by M.A.S. Abdel Haleem.

39 From the website Islam: Question and Answer; "The difference between major hypocrisy and minor hypocrisy", https://islamqa.info/en/153691 (accessed

Minor hypocrisy, which is also called *hypocrisy of actions*, refers to hypocrisy in deeds.

> That is when a person does righteous actions, but they do not truly represent what is in his heart, or he behaves differently in private and in public, but that does not have to do with the fundamentals of faith ...

It is recognized that minor hypocrisy may lead to major hypocrisy.

**Conclusion**

With their shared emphasis on law and traditions and on purity, both the Pharisees of Jesus´ day and the religious Muslims of our time, display a tendency towards legalism and a focus on external compliance. There it might be helpful to learn about how Jesus interacted with the Pharisees to follow His example in our interactions with religious Muslims.

---

December 22, 2021). The website Islam Question and Answer is supervised by Shaykh Muhammad Saalih al-Munajjid, from Saudi Arabia.

# CHAPTER 3
# JESUS' INTERACTION WITH THE PHARISEES

We have looked at the background of the Pharisees and learned that they were an influential group of about six thousand religious people, who were devoted to the Law of God in order to retain their (religious) identity in a multi/anti-religious, pluriform, hostile world. They had a desire to conform to the revealed will of God as made known in the law. Many Pharisees were lay religious teachers, who taught the law of God in the synagogues.

Most of the Pharisees were committed to spend their whole life observing every detail of the law of God. To them the law was the most sacred thing in all the world. Religion, for the Pharisees, was unimaginable without the law. They wanted to live a holy, righteous life, which for them consisted mostly in strict obedience to the law of God as being interpreted through their Traditions. They believed in life after death, the providence of God; they expected the coming of a Messiah to inaugurate the Kingdom of God.

Several of these characteristics are like those of the religious Muslims of our day. In the previous chapter we identified four similarities between the Pharisees of Jesus' day and modern day religious Muslims: a) emphasis on law and traditions; b) emphasis on purity; c) tendency towards legalism; d) tendency to focus on external compliance.

The way Jesus interacted with the Pharisees can be valuable lessons for those who want to engage with modern-day religious Muslims.

In this chapter I will look at how Jesus interacted with the Pharisees, particularly as we read about it in the Gospel of Luke. We can summarize Jesus' interaction with the Pharisees in this Gospel in three words: confrontation, condemnation, and compassion.

## Jesus' *confrontation* with the Pharisees

*"The collision between Pharisaism and Jesus is 'the mutual impact of two irreconcilable conceptions of religion'."*[40]

---

[40] R. Travers Herford, 208.

When studying the interactions between Jesus and the Pharisees, it becomes clear rather quickly that time and again there is strong disagreement between them.

Before we investigate this in more detail, it is important to not lose sight of the fact that both Jesus and the Pharisees were deeply committed to the revelation of God in the Torah. They both believed that the Torah was the Word of God, but they differed radically on how to interpret that Word.

This means that the disputes between Jesus and the Pharisees often had to do with the right interpretation of the Law of God. As we will see, this particularly applied to matters related to holiness (purity) and keeping the sabbath.

For the Pharisees, the basis for maintaining a pure and holy life, in relating to sinners, and in keeping the sabbath and many other life-style choices (e.g., fasting) was the law of God, the Torah.

> The conflict between the Pharisees and Jesus had been, in its essence, a conflict between two types of religion ... The religion of the Pharisees was expressed in terms of Torah: its central feature was an Idea, an intellectual as well as moral conception by means of which it defined and represented the relation of the human soul to God. The religion of Jesus was not expressed in terms of Torah and did not centre on an Idea. It was the outcome of his own immediate consciousness of God, apart from all forms of thought, apart from all traditional authority. ... The centre of gravity became Christ and not the Torah.[41]

Jesus said He had come not to abolish the Torah, but to fulfil it (Matthew 5:17). Through His life and in His death, He fulfilled the Torah's original intentions, namely a life of continuing obedience to God. In doing so, He changed the centre of gravity to Himself instead of the Torah. This brought Him into several confrontations with the Pharisees.

The ***confrontation*** between Jesus and the Pharisees particularly focused around the following issues:

- The identity of Jesus.
- What it means to be holy, pure before God, with regard to Table fellowship and Sabbath keeping.

---

[41] Ibid. 214.

### The identity of Jesus

*"Who is this who even forgives sins?"* (Luke 7:49)

Several times there was a confrontation between Jesus and the Pharisees about the topic of forgiveness (Luke 5:17–26; 7:36–50). The first time we read about the Pharisees in the Gospel of Luke, we see them as critical listeners and observers to Jesus healing a paralyzed man and forgiving his sins. The first words spoken by the Pharisees in Luke are found in 5:21 (actually, they were not even speaking it, but thinking it, but Jesus exposes their thoughts) had to do with His authority to forgive sins. Sometimes you get the impression that some Pharisees did not consider themselves as sinful and in need of forgiveness, because they kept to the law of God. Jesus did address this issue, as we will see, but one of the key issues in their confrontation with Jesus was: Who has the authority to forgiven sins? They wondered: *"Who is this fellow who speaks blasphemy? Who can forgive sins but God alone?"* (Luke 5:21)

For most Pharisees it was obvious that only God Himself can forgive. When Jesus forgives someone his sins, He seems to take on divine authority.

Later, we read that Jesus was invited to dinner by a Pharisee and because a woman who had lived a sinful life appeared in the gathering, the discussion between Jesus and his host turned around the topic of forgiveness and when Jesus told the sinful woman: *"Your sins are forgiven,"* the other guests (many of whom most likely were also Pharisees), began to say among themselves, *"Who is this who even forgives sins?"* (Luke 7:49)

Jesus' words were considered a clear, be it implicit, claim of divinity.

The identity of Jesus is an important topic in our contacts with Muslims. Most Muslims would accept the greatness of Jesus, but they would not accept His divinity.

> I read the whole New Testament, gospel after gospel ... Most of the teachings, especially those of Jesus, struck me with their admirable passion, devotion, sincerity, and godliness ... The only passages not to my liking were those that emphasized the divinity of Jesus – a belief that Islam's strict monotheism can never accept. ... To my Muslim mind, Jesus as a messenger of God was a very familiar, appealing theme. But Jesus as God was anathema.[42]

---

[42] Akyol, 2.

### What it means to be holy and pure

The second key aspect of Jesus' confrontation with the Pharisees relates to the question: "What does it meant to be holy and pure?"

This particularly comes out in two areas: table fellowship and keeping the sabbath.

### Holiness and purity regarding table fellowship

*"Why do you eat with tax collectors and sinners?"* (Luke 5:30)

Jesus' identity as the someone who calls sinners to repentance, and as a physician who heals the sick was not perceived by most of the Pharisees. This is also seen in how they respond to Jesus' table fellowship with sinners.

> The oriental ... would immediately understand the acceptance of the outcasts into table fellowship with Jesus as an offer of salvation to guilty sinners and as the assurance of forgiveness.[43]

Nevertheless, it is striking that Jesus appears not to require repentance in advance of having table fellowship with sinners. This might be the reason why the Pharisees assume that Jesus makes himself a social equal to the sinners.

They criticized Him because in their understanding He violated the ritual purity which, they believe, is important to maintain a right standing with God. The sinners with whom Jesus had table fellowship probably did not observe the dietary laws to which the Pharisees adhered.

While the Pharisees wanted to disassociate themselves from sinners to maintain their purity before God, we observe that Jesus association with the same sinners does not defile him.

> Jesus is not defiled by his contact with impurity but instead vanquishes it through the eschatological power active in him. We might thus speak of holiness for Jesus, rather than sin, being that which he views as contagious.[44]

---

43 Joachim Jeremias, quoted by Gowler, 202.

44 Blomberg, Craig L. *Contagious Holiness: Jesus' meals with sinners*, (Westmont, Illinois: InterVarsity Press, 2005), 102, 103.

### Holiness and purity regarding keeping the sabbath

*"Why are you doing what is unlawful on the Sabbath?"* (Luke 6:2)

The Pharisees' emphasis on purity before God did not only have consequences for their table fellowship, but also for the way they kept the Sabbath. The command of God: "to keep the Sabbath holy" was very important for them. This led to regular confrontations with Jesus (e.g., in Luke 6:1–10; 13:10–17; 14:1–6).

In the interest of keeping the Sabbath holy, as a day of rest, the Pharisees had expanded on the OT Sabbath laws, developing thirty-nine rules concerning activities forbidden on the Sabbath, which included reaping.[45]

Jesus healed on a Sabbath, picked grain on a Sabbath, threw out demons on a Sabbath. In doing so, he violated the Sabbath rules, at least in the understanding of the Pharisees.

> The sabbath, according to the Pharisees in Luke-Acts, is a sacred time that is related to other purity regulations. The way that Jesus neglects these social maps represents to the Pharisees a flagrant rejection of how God had ordered the world, and, more specifically, the purity regulations laid down by God's law. Jesus is contravening their entire God-ordained Weltanschauung. Thus, the Pharisees' objection is quite understandable; their mistake is that they do not recognize who Jesus is.[46]

In a rather unfriendly confrontation between Jesus and the Pharisees, resulting in the latter ones being furious and discussing in what they might do to Jesus, Jesus heals a man in a synagogue on a sabbath (Luke 6:6–10) Jesus is concerned for the man's condition, but the Pharisees seem to only be concerned about keeping their religious sabbath regulations.

> Jesus challenges the established system of purity. The Pharisees were concerned about the temporal purity regulation of the sabbath, whereas Jesus was concerned about the man with the withered hand. ... The man was living in a disvalued state of being, and Jesus was more

---

45 The Nazarene Way of Essenic Studies on their website: http://www.thenazareneway.com/sabbath/39_prohib_sabbath.htm (accessed March 18, 2021).

46 Gowler, 209, 210.

> concerned about him than about any sabbath rules. Thus Jesus provokes debate about the various purity rules; he questions the Pharisees' practice – as they question his – as well as the general social purpose of those rules. He emphatically declares that God's relationship to humanity and the resulting person-to-person relationships take precedence over purity rules – including sabbath observance.[47]

We have already seen that Pharisees emphasized purity. Their name 'Pharisee' is derived from the Hebrew word 'Parush' meaning 'separated' or 'isolated', in the sense of being holy and sanctified. They sought to strictly observe the Levitical purity and the avoidance of close association with anyone and anything impure.

It is therefore not surprising that in in the confrontation between Jesus and the Pharisees, the issue of purity predominates.

> Most of the conflicts between Jesus and the Pharisees in the Gospel of Luke are concerned with purity rules. Jesus often heals those who are unclean according to the purity rules and therefore are incapable of full social relationships or are barred from the Temple (8:43–48). Jesus even touches some of the unclean persons he heals (5:13). Such healings sometimes took place during a period of sacred time (i.e. on the Sabbath; 14:1–6), as well as in a sacred place during a period of sacred time (i.e. in the synagogue on the sabbath; Luke 6:6–11; 13:10–17). In addition, Jesus neglects to cleanse himself ritually before eating a meal (11:37, 38) and even eats with toll collectors and sinners (5:29,30). The Pharisees murmur in response (5:30). Thus, Jesus provokes debates about sacred persons, time and space; he questions the general social purpose of these rules and the way in which they were interpreted.[48]

Also, religious Muslims emphasize the importance of ritual purity and to maintain a 'halal-lifestyle'.

> Adopting a halal lifestyle is not only important for Muslims, but also for non-Muslims. It implies that the lifestyle we adopt and choose for ourselves is a considered one. It is a lifestyle that we are comfortable

---

[47] Ibid, 215.

[48] Gowler, 23.

with. We do not have any reservations, or guilt-feelings, or being embarrassingly apologetic about it, wherever we go or find ourselves drawn into it. If our choice of lifestyle is one of halal, then it affords us the opportunity to be accepted and respected by everyone else. Halal affords one the subconscious self-awareness of hygiene and health; safety and security; independence and self-determination. It is simply wholesome and awesome! Thus, our chosen halal lifestyle is an ethical one. It was a choice of lifestyle that was without force, discrimination, bias or prejudice. It would therefore be a chosen lifestyle that is pleasing to us, conducive and tolerable for all people and for every circumstance, place or venture. In essence, we have contentment-of-heart and an exemplary natural disposition towards others, as well. A halal lifestyle guarantees and manages the morality of whatever we do, say or become involved in. Once we have embraced such a halal lifestyle for ourselves, we would find happiness and contentment, as opposed to perplexity and anxiety in our lives. At the same time, it safeguards and preserves our dignity and honor; our self-respect and self-control; and our integrity and individuality. Maintaining a halal lifestyle offers us nothing else except equilibrium, modesty, sustainability, safety and stability in our lives. In essence, halal is a right of every Muslim, but it is indeed a privilege for every non-Muslim.[49]

## Jesus' *condemnation* of the Pharisees

We've seen that Jesus time and again was confronted by the Pharisees, or He confronted them. Although these confrontations might be explained as condemnations, perhaps they predominantly where challenges.

Nevertheless, Jesus does condemn the Pharisees with strong words. One of such incidents took place during a dinner in the house of a Pharisee (Luke 11:37–54).

Woe (alas) (ouai pronounced "oo-ah'ee", an eerie, ominous foreboding sound some say is like the cry of an eagle) is an onomatopoeic word (an

---

49 Muslim Judicial Council Halaal Trust (South Africa) on their website: https://mjchalaaltrust.co.za/education/importance-of-halal-lifestyle/ (accessed March 18, 2021).

> imitation of the sound) which serves as an interjection expressing a cry of intense distress, displeasure or horror. Jesus uses it to convey a warning of impending judgment and disaster on the Pharisees.

After a discussion about being ceremonially clean, versus having a clean heart (about which, see later), Jesus utters a series of three woes against the Pharisees and three more against the experts of the law, who most likely also belonged to the community of Pharisees.

### Jesus' six woes against the Pharisees

*The letter of the law had become more important than its spirit*

*"Woe to you Pharisees, because you give God a tenth of your mind, rue and all other kinds of garden herbs, but you neglect justice and the love of God. You should have practiced the latter without leaving the former undone."* (Luke 11:42)

The law of God required people to tithe (Leviticus 27:30–33; Deuteronomy 14:22–29; 2 Chronicles 31:5–12). Though tithing of everything from the land (grain, fruit, wine, olive oil) was required, the Pharisees seem to have interpreted tithing 'the seed of the land' to include even every kind of garden herb.

> They were meticulous on minutiae! They were punctilious regarding petty details! They majored on minors and minored on majors.[50]

With so much focus on the minute details of the letters of the law, they had become oblivious for the spirit of the law, that emphasizes justice and love. The prophets had warned about this:

> *He has told you, O man, what is good; And what does the LORD require of you But to do justice, to love kindness, And to walk humbly with your God?* (Micah 6:8)
>
> *Then the word of the LORD came to Zechariah saying, "Thus has the LORD of hosts said, "Dispense true justice and practice kindness and compassion each to his brother; and do not oppress the widow or the orphan, the stranger or the poor; and do not devise evil in your hearts against one another."* (Zechariah 7:8–10)

---

50 https://www.preceptaustin.org/luke-11-commentary (accessed March 18, 2021).

### *A good name had become more important than godliness*

*"Woe to you, Pharisees, because love the most important seats in the synagogues and respectful greetings in the marketplaces."* (Luke 11:43)

The second condemnation of Jesus to the Pharisees refers to their desire for publicity, prestige, honour of man, prominence, status and good reputation. This refers to an attitude of pride.

> The second woe spoken by Jesus ... His judgment of their actions – they love the best seats in the synagogue and salutations in the agoras – clearly portrays them as being greedy for social prominence ... Jesus declares that religious matters should not be used to enhance one's status in society.[51]

### *Appearance had become more important than character*

*"Woe to you, because you are like unmarked graves, which people walk over without knowing it."* (Luke 11:44)

In Jesus' third condemnation He compares the Pharisees to unseen graves. They emphasized holiness and purity, but for many Pharisees this seems to have been an outside veneer, not an inside reality. Holy appearance had replaced holy character. As a result, they caused others to become contaminated and unclean.

> The irony lies in the fact that the Pharisees were so concerned about purity, but they themselves cause uncleanness among those who come into contact with them. They had their true evil nature and lead unwitting persons astray.[52]

### *Preaching had become more important than practicing*

*"And you experts in the law, woe to you, because you load people down with burdens they can hardly carry, and you yourselves will not lift one finger to help them."* (Luke 11:46)

Jesus' fourth condemnation is directed to the experts of the law, many of them were Pharisees. These experts of the law were responsible for

---

[51] Gowler, 229.

[52] Ibid, 230.

teaching the Law of God to the people. In doing so they added their interpretations, rules and regulations, which they taught others to observe, and they put these as burdens on others.

> The lawyers ought to have expounded God's Law in such a way that it helped and inspired people. Instead they made it a wearisome burden.[53]

Not only did they make the Law of God into a burdensome task, which is almost impossible for people to carry out, they found loopholes for themselves to not do what they preached to others to do.

> The lawyers had taken the commands of Scripture and had multiplied them into hundreds of minute adaptations. But, like lawyers in every age, they had also come up with legal loopholes that enabled them to skirt around their own rules, while the average guy was still burdened with them.[54]

### *Paying lip-service had become more important than obedience*

*"Woe to you, because you build tombs for the prophets, and it was your ancestors who killed them."* (Luke 11:47)

The fifth condemnation of Jesus refers to the way the experts of the Law related to the prophets of the past. These prophets were sent by God and often criticized the people of God for not obeying the Law of God. Because they didn't like the message, the people of the past killed the messenger. By building their tombs, the experts of the Law gave the impression that they admired the prophets who were buried there. It looked like they honoured them, but at the same time they did not submit to their message, and they did not repent of the sins these prophets condemned. Instead of building their tombs they should have listened to their message. Jesus points out that because of they haven't listened the judgment of God will come upon them.

> Jesus is saying that the blood of all the righteous men who were martyred in the Old Testament would be charged against this current

---

53 Morris, Leon. *Luke,* The Tyndale NT Commentaries, (Grand Rapids: Wm. B. Eerdmans, 1974), 225.

54 Steve Cole https://bible.org/seriespage/lesson-57-why-jesus-hates-legalism-luke-1137-54 (accessed March 18, 2021).

> wicked generation, because they rejected God's revealed wisdom about their sin. This may point to the awful judgment on Jerusalem in A.D. 70 or it may also include the final judgment. The point is, legalists don't apply God's holiness to their hearts; they just put on an outward show of honoring it.[55]

*Religious expertise had become more important than knowing God*

*"Woe to you experts in the law, because you have taken away the key to knowledge. You yourselves have not entered, and you have hindered those who were entering."* (Luke 11:52)

The final condemnation that Jesus directs at the experts of the law/pharisees is that instead of helping people come closer to God, they actually hindered them from knowing Him as He reveals himself in Scriptures. Their man-made rules and their elaborate regulations made the Word of God, the true source of knowing God, into a mystery book that can only be understood by religious experts.

> Their methods were such that people could not get at the essential meaning of God's word. Instead of opening up the treasures of knowledge, the lawyers closed them fast. They turned the Bible into a book of obscurities, a bundle of riddles which only the experts could understand. And the experts were so pleased and preoccupied with the mysteries they had manufactured that they missed the wonderful thing that God was saying. They neither entered themselves nor allowed others to enter. There were ordinary people on their way to the knowledge of God until these teachers turned them away.[56]

As a result of these condemnations, which all in one way or another refer to the fact that many Pharisees mistakenly made serving God predominantly an outward matter, instead of a heart issue, the Pharisees and lawyers "began to oppose him fiercely and besiege Him with questions, waiting to catch him in something he might say." (Luke 11:53, 54)

---

[55] Steve Cole https://bible.org/seriespage/lesson-57-why-jesus-hates-legalism-luke-1137-54 (accessed March 18, 2021).

[56] Morris, 226.

Nevertheless, Jesus not only confronts and condemns them, but also invites them with compassion. We'll look at this now.

## Jesus' *compassion* for the Pharisees

*"So his father went out and pleaded with him ... 'My son,' the father said, 'you are always with me, and everything I have is yours' ..."* (Luke 15:28–31)

Not only did Jesus confront and condemn the Pharisees as we have seen, but He also showed *compassion* for them.

> The Pharisees regularly receive condemnation from Jesus (e.g., Luke 11:37–54), but sometimes a call to repentance is included in those attacks (Luke 14:14; 15:3–32).[57]

This comes particularly through in some of the parables that Jesus addresses to them. For example, when Jesus ate in the house of a Pharisee, he told them the story of the great banquet, in which "a certain man prepared a great banquet and invited many guests, with the words: everything is now ready." (Luke 14:15–24). Unfortunately, many of the invitees did not accept this gracious invitation. The implication seems to be that the Pharisees were among the first invitees to eat at the feast in the Kingdom of God, but many of them declined.

One of the parables that shows Jesus' compassion for the Pharisees, is the Parable of the Prodigal son that we find in Luke 15:11–31.

After the Pharisees again complained about Jesus welcoming and eating with sinners (15:2)[58], Jesus directed three parables to them: the parable of the lost sheep, the lost coin and the lost son. These parables emphasize the joy of God over the lost being found. God rejoices when those who have walked away from Him, return to His heart and house.

The parable that is one of the most known parables of Jesus is often known as 'the parable of the prodigal son'. Nevertheless, the parable speaks about ***two*** sons of the father. From the context in which the parable is spoken, is becomes clear that the prodigal son represents the sinners: people who have clearly disrespected the father (God), have abused His wealth for their

---

[57] Gowler, 257.

[58] This was a recurring complaint, see also Luke 5:30; 7:30; 19:7.

personal gain and to gratify their sinful desires. When these people come to their senses and embark on a way back to the father, they discover the father welcomes them with open arms, forgives their sins, provides them with identity and dignity and throws a great party, because he is overjoyed for the return of the prodigal son.

But the other son, the older son also plays a significant role in this parable. It must have been obvious for the first listeners that as the younger son represented the sinners, the older brother represented the Pharisees.

The older son compared himself with his younger brother, the sinner, and justified himself with the words: *"I have been slaving for you and never disobeyed your orders."* (Luke 15:29) He considered himself a righteous man because of his obedience to the orders of the father. This coincides with a desire to be righteous according to Law and the tendency to legalism that we have observed earlier among many Pharisees of Jesus' day. The oldest son also defines his relationship with his father first and foremost of that of *servant* instead of that of *son*. This is an example of someone who makes religion into a task instead of a relationship. A further similarity between the behaviour of the oldest son and that of the Pharisees is an emphasis on holiness based on outward appearance, while ignoring the sinfulness of his disrespectful behaviour towards his father. Another similarity between this oldest son and the Pharisees is his judgmental and condescending attitude towards his sinful brother, whom he no longer regarded as a brother, and to whom he refers as 'this son of yours.'

Having identified several similarities between the eldest son in the parable of Jesus and the Pharisees, it is very interesting to see how the father (God) treats this other son of His.

I want to note four things:

- **He took the initiative for the restoring of the relationship**; The father, who had been running to welcome his prodigal son, *"went out"* (Luke 15: 28) to his other son. He went out of his way to also meet with the son, who had also hurt him by his behaviour. The father took the initiative to welcome his older son to the party.
- **He sought to convince him of his love and forgiveness**; We read *"he pleaded with him"* (Luke 15: 28). This son had hurt the father and disrespected him in front of others by not coming to the celebra-

tions. Later we read some of the words that the father used to convince his son that he was more than welcome. The father wanted to convince the son of his love and compassion for him. It must have been clear for the listeners that God loved both sons and wanted both to celebrate His goodness.

- **He identified him as a son**. The father addresses the older brother as *"My son."* (Luke 15:31) The older brother saw himself as a servant of the father and seems to have lost sight of the fact that although he worked for the father, he was first of all a 'son'. The older brother, the Pharisee, needed to remind himself who he was in the eyes of God.
- **He reassured him of his place.** The father said: *"You are always with me and everything I have is yours."* (Luke 15:31) The return of his younger brother did in no way diminish his own standing and his portion of the father's wealth.

The parable clearly shows the love of God for both sinners and Pharisees, who are also sinners of course. Both hear the invitation of the father to join His celebrations, both hear of His love and forgiveness, both are given identity and wealth. The foundation of this generous offer of God is His grace. It might be easier to accept grace, when you have come to the end of your rope as the youngest son experienced, then when you are slaving for years and in your understanding have 'never disobeyed an order', as the older son expressed. We know how the youngest son responded, but the response of the eldest son is not given. Will he join the celebration? The Pharisees objected to Jesus' welcoming sinners into God's family. Was it because they didn't consider themselves helpless sinners, who could only be accepted by God through grace? Was it because they thought their obedience to the law was a means of acceptance by God instead of an expression of their thankfulness for being accepted?

Although Jesus frequently confronted the Pharisees, particularly regarding His authority to forgive sins and His interpretation of what it means to be holy and pure; and although Jesus condemned the Pharisees, particularly their emphasis on external religion instead of heart connection with God, He did warmly and wholeheartedly invite them to participate in God's salvation. Some have responded to Jesus' compassionate invitation as we will see later.

If we as followers of Christ want to follow Him in our interactions with religious Muslims, who in many ways resemble the Pharisees of Jesus' time, we might need to confront their understanding of the identity of Jesus and their perception of holiness and purity. There might also be times when we have to clearly criticize their prioritizing letter over spirit, good name over godliness, appearance over character, preaching over practicing, lip-service over obedience or expertise over knowing. Nevertheless, let us also follow our Lord and Saviour to confront and condemn not with hardness of heart or of a cold argumentative spirit, but with a compassion so that in all our interactions with them they get a glimpse of the merciful and gracious Lord we serve.

# CHAPTER 4
# JESUS' LESSONS TO THE PHARISEES THAT ARE APPLICABLE TO MUSLIMS

*"... I believe that the teachings of Jesus to his fellow Jews can today give us Muslims reformist guidance especially in two key matters. The first is the Kingdom of God, which Muslims would call the Caliphate. The second is religious law, which Muslims would call the Shariah."*[59]

We have seen that we can draw out some parallels between the Pharisees that Jesus dealt with and the religious Muslims of our day. Jesus confronted their wrong interpretation of the law, condemned their hypocrisy and invited them to join the divine banquet. In this invitation to participate of God's grace, goodness and forgiveness, Jesus shared the Gospel with them. In this chapter we will look at how Jesus framed the Gospel message for the Pharisees in order to learn how we can do this in our contacts with the religious Muslims of our day.

I will particularly look at:

- The kingdom of God is first of all a spiritual reality
- Purity before God is first of all a matter of the heart
- Righteousness before God not a path, but a present

## The Kingdom of God is first of all a spiritual reality

*"Once, on being asked by the Pharisees when the kingdom of God would come, he replied, "The coming of the kingdom of God is not something that can be observed, nor will people say, 'Here it is', or 'There it is,' because the Kingdom of God is in your midst.""* (Luke 17:21)

The Pharisees, like other religious Jews at the time of Jesus, were eagerly looking for and expecting the coming of the eschatological Kingdom of God, as foretold by their prophets. In their understanding this kingdom would be inaugurated by the Messiah, who would defeat the enemies of God and set

59 Akyol, 206.

up God's eternal kingly rule resulting in eternal peace, righteousness and glory.

> ..throughout all Judaism, the coming of God's Kingdom was expected to be an act of God – perhaps using the agency of men – to defeat the wicked enemies of Israel and to gather Israel together, victorious over her enemies, in her promised land, under the rule of God alone.[60]

Jesus spoke about the Kingdom of God very often. In fact, he defined His ministry in terms related to the Kingdom of God, when He said: *"I must proclaim* ***the good news of the kingdom of God*** *to the other towns also, because that is why I was sent." (Luke 4:42).*

He preached the Good News of the kingdom of God (Luke 16:16). He spoke parables to explain the secrets of kingdom of God (Luke 8:10; 13:18,20). He mentioned that several people would not die before they saw the kingdom of God (Luke 9:27). He referred to being fit for service in the kingdom of God (Luke 9:62). He encouraged His disciples to pray "Your kingdom come." (Lukas 11:2) and to seek God's kingdom (Luke 12:31). He emphasized that God is pleased to give the kingdom to Jesus's disciples (Lukas 12:32), and that the kingdom of God belongs to those who are like children (Luke 18:16,17). He said that the miracles He performed (such as casting out demons) where a sign that the kingdom of God has come (Luke 11:20). He mentioned about people being invited to the feast in God's kingdom, while others would be thrown out (Luke 13:28–30: 14:15–24). People who give up riches or relationships because of the kingdom of God will be rewarded (Luke 18:29). In answer to the question from His disciples he spoke about signs that will show that the kingdom of God is near (Luke 21:31). Prior to His death He referred to the kingdom as 'my kingdom' and said to His disciples: "And I confer on you a kingdom, just as my Father conferred one on me, so that you may eat and drink at my table in my kingdom and sit on thrones ..." (Luke 22:29,30)

Given the fact that the Pharisees, along with many Jews of that day were eagerly anticipating the coming of the kingdom of God, it is no wonder that they paid good attention to Jesus, who gave this kingdom such a prominent place in his message and ministry. As a result of Jesus' words and ministry

---

[60] Ladd, George Eldon. *A Theology of the New Testament* (Grand Rapids: Wm. B. Eerdmans, 1959), 63.

of miracles, some people thought "that the kingdom of God was going to appear at once." (Luke 19:11)

While both Jesus and the Pharisees were deeply interested in the kingdom of God, there was huge difference between them about *the identity of this kingdom* and Jesus has to correct their misunderstanding.

First of all, He ***universalized*** the concept of Kingdom of God. Among Jews the Kingdom of God was pictured in terms of *Israel,* but Jesus made it clear that all those who respond to *Him* in a positive way and childlike attitude, from east, west, north and south, would be part of the Kingdom of God (Luke 13:28–30; 14:15–24; 18:16,17). Jesus de-nationalized the concept of the Kingdom of God and made entrance into it dependent not upon one's ethnic background, but upon one's commitment to the future King of this Kingdom, namely Jesus Christ Himself.

The second difference in understanding between the Pharisees and Jesus regarding the Kingdom of God is that Jesus ***internalized*** the Kingdom of God. While not denying the fact that there will be a future earthly Kingdom of God, under the leadership of God Himself, an eternity of peace, joy and righteousness, Jesus emphasized that the Kingdom of God is something that one can here and now become part of, once God rules in one's soul. The words of Luke 17:21: "... the kingdom of God is in your midst", can also be translated "the kingdom of God is within you." This doesn't mean that the kingdom of God is automatically in us, nor that the kingdom of God was already in the Pharisees that Jesus was speaking to.

The kingdom of God exists in the hearts of all those who accept Jesus Christ as King of their lives. In those people, God through His holy Spirit takes residence and these people become 'people of the kingdom'.

> The Kingdom of God is the dynamic rule of God active in Jesus; it is also present realm of blessing into which men enter who receive Jesus' word.[61]

---

[61] Ladd, 72.

The internal Kingdom that Jesus spoke about was to be erected in the hearts of man, consisting in the subjection of their wills to the will of God, and in the conformity of their minds to His laws.[62]

Those who have become people of the Kingdom, seek to live according to the principles and values of this Kingdom. Although the full realization of the Kingdom of God is future, the Kingdom does manifest itself in the present already, there where Jesus' presence is celebrated and the power of the Spirit active through healing, liberation and reconciliation.

Jesus emphasized the 'already and not yet paradigm' of the kingdom of God. The Pharisees were waiting for the signs of a visible kingdom. They had wrongly interpreted the OT eschatology, especially regarding earth shaking signs. But Jesus emphasized that the before the kingdom of God becomes a visible kingdom, it is a spiritual kingdom. One can enter into it and experience its gifts and blessings already in the present, while waiting for its future consummation in fullness.

The Pharisees assumed, based on Jesus' words and actions, that He implied that He was the King of the *visible* kingdom they were looking for. And of course, they were correct that Jesus was the King, but they did not understand that first He had to be received by faith as King of their hearts, King of an *invisible*, internal kingdom, before they could truly see and become part of the future visible kingdom.

Ladd summarizes Jesus' teaching of the Kingdom of God as follows:

> Thus the unforeseen presence of the eschatological salvation is illustrated in many aspects of Jesus' message and mission and is to be seen far beyond the actual terminology of the Kingdom of God. The mission of Jesus brought not a new teaching but a new event. It brought men and actual foretaste of the eschatological salvation. Jesus did not promise the forgiveness of sins; he bestowed it. He did not simply assure men of the future fellowship of the Kingdom; he invited men into fellowship with himself as the bearer of the Kingdom. He did not merely promise them vindication in the day of judgment; he bestowed upon them a present righteousness. He not only taught an

---

[62] Benson, Joseph. *Commentary of the Old and New Testaments* (New York: T. Carlton & J. Porter, 1857). http://biblehub.com (accessed March 18, 2021).

> eschatological deliverance from physical evil; he went about demonstrating the redeeming power of The Kingdom, delivering men from sickness and even death. This is the meaning of the presence of the Kingdom as a new era of salvation. To receive the Kingdom of God, to submit oneself to God's reign meant to receive the gift of the Kingdom and to enter into the enjoyment of its blessings. The age of fulfilment is present, but the time of consummation still awaits the Age to Come.[63]

Like the Pharisees of Jesus' day, many Muslims of today are eagerly expecting the future rule of God, which they call the Caliphate. For many Muslims such Caliphate is a theocracy that will bring glory to the umma (the global community of Muslims).

> Some Muslims are merely hoping to see the Caliphate established as a distant utopia, and they can be classified as "conservatives." Others are more engaged and actively work for the utopia through political action, which earns them the label "Islamists." Then there is a small minority that opts for armed struggle, which makes them "jihadists." And among these jihadists, only the most radical fringe, ISIS, declared a "Caliphate" in 2014, something that looks too militant for the overwhelming majority of Muslims.[64]

Like the Pharisees, these Muslims will need to hear that the kingdom of God is not first of all *a geo-political entity* to be realized in the here and now, but *a spiritual entity* that one can enter only when one has committed his or her life into the hands of this future King, namely Jesus Christ. Religious Muslims need to hear the Good News of the Kingdom of God that Jesus proclaimed.

If Akyol is right, these words might fall on fertile ground:

> ... it is possible for Muslims today to abandon the commitment to the Caliphate as a political entity , but strive to be better caliphs on earth – as individuals with God-given faculties and responsibilities. It is possible for Muslims to think, in other words, that the Caliphate is not here or there, but within themselves.[65]

---

63 Ladd, 80.

64 Akyol, 208.

65 Akyol, 210.

## Purity before God is first of all a matter of the heart

*"Now then, you Pharisees clean the outside of the cup and dish, but inside you are full of greed and wickedness. You foolish people! Did not the one who made the outside make the inside also? But now as for what is inside you -be generous to the poor, and everything will be clean for you."* (Luke 11:40)

The second aspect of the Good News that Jesus spoke to the Pharisees and that is important in our conversation with religious Muslims of our time is that purity before God is first of all a matter of the heart.

The call of God to His people of all times is: ´Be Holy, as I am Holy` This call comes with several practical guidelines for one´s daily life. Particularly the book of Leviticus has a lot to say about what it means to be ceremonially clean or unclean in the eyes of the Lord. It relates to the food one eats, one's body (e.g., pregnancy, monthly periods, skin diseases, certain discharges). It extended to mould on clothes, touching unclean or dead people and animals, sexual relationships etc.[66]

We have already seen that the Pharisees emphasized purity. Even their name 'Pharisee' is derived from the Hebrew word 'Parush' meaning 'separated' or 'isolated', in the sense of being holy and sanctified.

The Pharisees sought to strictly observe the Levitical purity and the avoidance of close association with anyone and anything impure.

> Faced with social, political and cultural 'pollution' at the level of national life as a whole, one natural reaction ... was to concentrate on personal cleanness, to cleanse and purify an area over which one did have control as a compensation for the impossibility of cleansing or purifying an area – the outward and visible political one – over which one had none. ... The Pharisees tried to maintain purity at a degree higher than that prescribed in the Hebrew Bible for ordinary Jews under ordinary conditions ...[67]

Their concept of purity applied to things, persons, places and times. Certain places, peoples, times and things were considered more holy or pure than others. Also, certain times, people, places and things convey uncleanness

---

66 See particularly Leviticus chapters 11-15.

67 Wright, 189–195.

and could make a person unclean by contact. A purity-conscious group like the Pharisees created boundaries between themselves and things, places, people and times that were considered impure, or unclean. They kept away from lepers or people with defective bodies. They could not share space, let alone a meal, with people who were considered sinners. They clearly separated between holy times during which one shouldn't work (like sabbath) and other times. With such a strong sense of clean and unclean, it is no surprise that attention is predominantly given to boundaries and margins.

In the eyes of the Pharisees Jesus violated their concept of purity. For example, He travelled through the unclean territory of Samaritans (Luke 9:51). He had dealings with 'unclean' Gentiles (Luke 8:26–37). He consorted with unclean demon-possessed people in a cemetery (8:28–31. He healed a Samaritan (Luke 17:16). He touched dead people (Luke 7:11–17; 8:49–56), who were considered unclean. He shared meals with the morally unclean people, who ate unclean food (Luke 5:27–32; 7:29; 31–34; 15:1–2; 18:4–14; 19:1–10). He permitted being touched by a public sinful woman (Luke 5:8–10) and a menstruating woman (Luke 8:42–48). He touched a leper (Luke 5:13) The bodily unholy (e.g., blind, cripples, sick, demon-possessed) were objects of Jesus' ministry. (Luke 4:31–37; 4:38–40; 5:17–26; 7,21; 8:26–29) and in fact he encouraged the Pharisees to invite such people for their banquets, because in His understanding that's how things are in the kingdom of God (Luke 14:12–21). Jesus did not seem to care much about the sacred times and rules that Pharisees had associated with these (e.g., Sabbath, fasting; Luke 6:1–11; 13:10–17; 5:33–35). Also, Jesus did not regard the dietary laws (Luke 9:10–17; 10:7,8).

Although Jesus was interested in purity and did abide by the Divine rule "Be Holy, as I am Holy, and although He even was referred to as 'the Holy One'." (Luke 2:35), He disagreed with the Pharisees about the *kind of purity*, which in Jesus' understanding was first a matter of *the heart* and only then of *the hand.*

This difference of understanding of purity between Jesus and the Pharisees came to the front when Jesus had lunch with a Pharisee. The Pharisee was surprised that Jesus did not first wash before the meal. Being ceremonially clean was very important for this Pharisee and many of his comrades. In another incident on this topic, which is recorded in the Gospel of Mark, we get the following additional information:

> *The Pharisees and all the Jews do not eat unless they give their hands a ceremonial washing, holding to the tradition of the elders. When they come from the marketplace they do not eat unless they wash.* (Mark 7:3,4)

The washing of the hands was done not just to get rid of germs, but to make oneself clean of impure things or people that one might have touched during the day.

Jesus apparently had broken one of the Pharisees religious traditions and this didn't go unnoticed. Instead of apologizing for his inappropriate behaviour, Jesus turns this incident into an important spiritual lesson.

He basically asked: "If you serve your guest drink and food, you make sure that the cup and plate are clean, but what would this matter if you then would put poison in the cup or on the plate?"

Jesus then applies this same principle to someone's body and soul. *External cleanness* is good, but *internal cleanness* is essential. Jesus responded by making a connection between the exteriors being cleansed and the internal situations were being ignored. He emphasized that a clean heart is more important than a clean plate! The Pharisees may have had clean dishes, but they also had dirty hearts!

With all their emphasis on *external* purity, which dominated their daily lives not only with regard to food, but also with regard to time (Sabbath) and people (whom to associate with), they had apparently lost sight of the need to seek and maintain *internal* purity, by getting rid of sin, such as greed and all kinds of wickedness.

Purity of heart would come out in one's behaviour, for example in how one conducts its religious duties, such as almsgiving.

> Jesus seems to be saying that if we deal with our hearts before God, then everything that flows outward is clean. As J. C. Ryle explains, "Give first the offering of the inward man. Give your heart, your affections, and your will to God, as the first great alms which you bestow, and then all your other actions, proceeding from a right heart, are an acceptable sacrifice, and a clean offering in the sight of God" (Cole)[68]

---

[68] https://www.preceptaustin.org/luke-11-commentary (accessed March 18, 2021).

Just as the Pharisees would agree with the proverb, *"Cleanliness is next to godliness"*[69] religious Muslims stress the importance of cleanliness and purification. Making purity ('Tahara' in Arabic) is an essential part of the Islamic faith. One of the Hadith states that Muhammad said: *"Cleanliness is half the faith (Emaan)."*[70]

We have already noted earlier that religious Muslims strongly emphasize purity. One of the ways many Muslims believe they can purify themselves is through performing the 'Zakat' (almsgiving). The word 'Zakat' comes from an Arabic word that is related to purification.

On their website, the UK based National Zakat Foundation clearly links almsgiving with purification:

> When we pay our Zakat, we purify our wealth and it apparently seems to diminish. But in reality, this purification paves the way for growth, as Allah blesses our wealth and our endeavours. ... So, if and when you pay your Zakat this Ramadan, remember that you are not only completing the most important pillar in Islam after the five daily prayers. You are also engaging in a beautiful act of purification, both of yourself and your wealth. You are paving the way for your prosperity in this life and the next.[71]

In his discussion with the Pharisees, Jesus also refers to almsgiving in the context of purification. Almsgiving is not to be interpreted as the above-mentioned Muslims seem to do, to be purified, but as a ***consequence*** of a pure heart that comes from a right relationship with God.

> In Jewish culture giving alms to the poor was a very important religious observance; it was meant to be an act of mercy, kindness, and love (D. L. Bock, Luke [BECNT], 2:1114). The implication from the text is that the Pharisees gave alms, but without any of the spiritual

---

69 See Mishnah, Soṭah, ix. 15.

70 Sahih Muslim, The Book of Purification, hadith 223. Sahih Muslim is a collection of hadith compiled by Imam Muslim ibn al-Hajjaj al-Naysaburi (rahimahullah). His collection is considered to be one of the most authentic collections of the Sunnah of the Muhammad.

71 The National Zakat Foundation in the UK on their website: https://www.nzf.org.uk/blog/zakat-pay-purify-prosper-protect-by-iqbal-nasim (accessed March 18, 2021).

> concern which should have motivated those generous actions. Here Jesus commands the Pharisees to give from within themselves to those in need instead of just giving of their possessions. In so doing they would show true inner purity acceptable to God. ... The expression everything ***will be clean for you*** refers to the agreement that should exist between the overt practice of one's religious duties, such as almsgiving, and the inner condition of one's heart, including true love for God and the poor; one is not only to wash the outside of the cup and plate, but the inside as well, since as Jesus said, God created the inside too. Religious duties are not to be performed hypocritically, i.e., for the applause and esteem of people, but rather they are to be done out of a deep love for God and a sensitivity to and concern for the needs of others. Then, everything will be clean, both hearts and lives.[72]

The message that Jesus spoke to the Pharisees and that religious Muslims need to hear is that what matters most in our relationship with God is that our hearts are pure. It is the pure in heart that will see God, Jesus said.[73] Purity of heart is not something a person can accomplish through our (religious) deeds. We can never purify our own hearts. A pure heart is a gift from the Sovereign God given to those who put their faith in Him and trust in the provision He made for their eternal salvation through the life and death of Jesus Christ.

## Righteousness before God is not a path but a present

*"What must I do to inherit eternal life?"* (Luke 10:25)

For the Pharisees, the basis for maintaining a pure and holy life, in relating to sinners, and in keeping the sabbath and many other life-style choices (e.g., fasting washing of hands and cups) was the law of God. Their reference point for conducting their life here and now and also regarding life eternal, was the law of God. It is therefore not a surprise that when an expert in the law, who most likely came from among the Pharisees, asked him: "What must I do to inherit eternal life?" Jesus referred him to the law.

---

72 NET Bible Notes, on https://www.preceptaustin.org/luke-11-commentary (accessed March 18, 2021).

73 One of the beatitudes, Matthew 5:8.

The lawyer knew the Old Testament and quoted Deuteronomy 6:5 (part of the Jewish Shema, which was repeated twice a day by devout Jews) and Leviticus 19:18. In so doing he answered the question in the same way Jesus Himself did when He was asked about the greatest commandment in the Law.[74]

> The command calls for total commitment to selfless love ... involving all human faculties, including the heart, soul, strength, and mind. These two commands sum up the Ten Commandments, the first half of which describes how to love God, while the second half describes how to love one's neighbor.[75]

The answer the man gave was correct and this showed that he was not far from the kingdom of God,[76] but 'not far away' is not the same as 'in'. In fact, it seems that this man was walking in the wrong direction, as becomes clear when the conversation goes on.

Jesus then urges the lawyer: "Do this and you will live."(Luke 10:28) With these words, Jesus wanted to make clear that perfect obedience to the law was not possible. At this point the lawyer should have realized the incompatibility of his words "do" and "inherit eternal life" that were mentioned in in his question: "What must I do to inherit eternal life?" In order to inherit eternal life, one should keep the law perfectly all the time, which no man is able to do.

> At first, it might appear that the Lord was teaching salvation by law-keeping. Such was not the case. God never intended that anyone should ever be saved by keeping the law. The Ten Commandments were given to people who were already sinners. The purpose of the law is not to save from sin, but to produce the knowledge of sin. The function of the law is to show man what a guilty sinner he is.[77]

The scribe should have realized that salvation by works is impossible and should have asked to be given eternal life as a gracious gift from a holy and righteous God, who forgives everyone who puts their trust in Jesus.

---

74 Mt 22:35–40; Mk 12:28–31.

75 John MacArthur, http://www.preceptaustin.org/luke-10-commentary (accessed March 18, 2021).

76 Mark 12:34.

77 MacDonald, William. *Believer's Bible Commentary* (Nashville: Thomas Nelson, 2016)

Instead of acknowledging that justification is a gracious gift, the man wanted to justify himself. Instead of saying: "If this is what God requires, then I'm lost, helpless, and hopeless. I cast myself on Your love and mercy. Save me by Your grace!" he wanted to continue on the road of good works and self-righteousness. He wanted to bring himself into a right relationship with God and asked: "And who is my neighbour?" He thought he only needed more guidance: some criteria to define the term 'neighbour'.

Although Jesus responded by telling the famous parable of the Good Samaritan, He didn't really answer the question: "Who is my neighbour?" but made the man look at himself and reflecting on the question: For whom am I a neighbour?

The characters in the parable (priest, Levite, Samaritan) are not chosen randomly. The priest and the Levite represented people, much like the scribe, who followed the law to become righteous. The Samaritan was an outsider, someone whom most Pharisees did not want to associate with in order not to defile themselves.

> The man had asked, 'Who is my neighbour?' but Jesus faced him with the question 'To whom am I neighbour?' He was an expert in the Law. Now he must think whether the priest and the Levite, who scrupulously retained the moral purity required by the Law, really kept the Law, which likewise enjoined love of the neighbour.[78]

The lawyer understood that the one who had mercy on a fellow human being in need, irrespective of cause, culture and circumstance, was the one who loves his neighbour as himself. Unfortunately, the law-abiding people tend to be more interested in maintaining their purity in order to show their love of God, than to live up to God's standard in relation to fellow human beings.

> Obviously, Christ's point is that neither the scribe nor anyone else is capable of such love. This is an indictment of the whole of fallen humanity, and the only proper response was for him to acknowledge his inability to save himself, and plead with God for mercy and forgiveness. Jesus, God incarnate, stood before him ready to extend

---

[78] Leon Morris, http://www.preceptaustin.org/luke-10-commentary (accessed March 18, 2021).

> forgiveness, grace, and mercy to him. But there is no indication that the lawyer did so; his pride and self-righteousness held him captive and he likely forfeited eternal life.[79]

How tragic, someone who knew the right way to inherit eternal life, missed it because he was unwilling to open his hands for the grace of God.

The law of God was a key aspect of the life of Pharisees, as it defined the path they wanted to walk on in their pursuit of righteousness and acceptance by the Almighty God. With their emphasis on strict outward obedience to the Law of God they had a false sense of righteousness, of a right standing before God; many of them didn't see themselves as sinners in need for repentance (Luke 18:9–14), nor did they realize their blindness (John 9:40, 41) nor their need of a doctor (Luke 5:27–31).

Likewise, among religious Muslims, the law of God, referred to as Shariah, plays a significant role in their desire to serve the Almighty God. The word 'Sharia' conveys the idea of a 'path to a well'. Sharia has been defined as follows:

> It is the absolute cure for all ills. ... It is life and nutrition, the medicine, the light, the cure and the safeguard. Every good in this life is derived from it and achieved through it, and every deficiency in existence results from its dissipation. ... If God wished to destroy the world and dissolve existence, He would void whatever remains of its injunctions. For the sharia ... is the pillar of existence and the key to success in this world and the Hereafter.[80]

*"Righteousness is not that you turn your faces toward the east or the west, but [true] righteousness is [in] one who believes in God, the Last Day, the angels, the Book, and the prophets and gives wealth, in spite of love for it, to relatives, orphans, the needy, the traveler, those who ask [for help], and for freeing slaves; [and who] establishes prayer and gives zakah (obligatory charity); [those who] fulfill their promise when they promise; and [those who] are patient in poverty and ailment and during battle. Those are the ones who have been true, and it is those who are the righteous."* (Surah 2:177)[81]

---

79 MacArthur, ibid.

80 A 14th-century Syrian jurist named Ibn Qayyim, quoted on http://islam.ru/en/content/story/sharia-path-salvation (accessed March 18, 2021)

81 "The Qur'an", translation by Sahih International.

This verse is often referred to as "the verse of righteousness". It points out that righteousness if found in those who believe in God and other beliefs and perform certain deeds. Righteousness (Arabic: Birr) consists of believe in God, to do good acts that please God and to behave well towards others.

> You shall not attain righteousness until you spend out of what you love (in the way of Allah). Allah knows whatever you spend. (Surah 3:92)[82]

> Righteousness is in good character, and wrongdoing is that which wavers in your soul, and which you dislike people finding about it. (Hadith)

Muslims are encouraged to realize the "righteous path of God, but many realize it entails an ongoing moral struggle to attain this path of righteousness, which is considered a divine path. Because only God knows the righteous path, Muslims are encouraged to pray: "Guide us to the straight path." (Sura 1:6)[83]

Although it is admitted that no one is able to fully and always attain righteousness, many Muslims are encouraged to keep pursuing this path to the best of their ability.

> Elements of the righteous path – or, in other words, basic moral precepts – are accessible to human beings through the act of diligent remembrance and reflection or even by an honest willingness to open one's heart to the reprimands of a critical intuitive conscience.[84]

Shariah is the divinely appointed path that religious Muslims seek to walk in order to come into the eternal presence of God, who is the Source of all Goodness. As such Shariah is considered a path to salvation. It is the supreme expression of righteousness.

> According to Muslim legal theory, the purpose of Islamic law is to seek after the righteous path – to try to come as close as possible to it, and in doing so achieve the welfare of the people.[85]

---

[82] "The Qur'an", translation by Abul Ala Maududi.

[83] "The Qur'an", translation by M.A.S. Abdel Haleem.

[84] Khaled Abou El Fadl, https://www.abc.net.au/religion/living-in-the-light-of-god-islamic-law-and-ethical-obligation/10100004 (accessed March 18, 2021).

[85] Ibid.

# CHAPTER 5
# JESUS' WAYS OF REACHING OUT TO THE PHARISEES

The majority of the Pharisees of Jesus' day were committed, religious people, who served God through their obedience to the law of Moses; they stressed morality and purity. Some of them were teachers. They were familiar with the revealed truth of God.

Most of them did not consider themselves to be sinners in need of forgiveness, or sick and in need of a healer. They thought that their religious activities and morals made them acceptable to God. They considered themselves to be righteous and not in need of repentance. Many Pharisees were constantly aware of sin around them and therefore strictly kept purity laws and did not associate with people whom they considered sinners.

As a result, many Pharisees were judgmental, lacked a proper understanding of grace; looked down on sinners and did not want to associate with them. They were legalists who squeezed mercy out of their lives.

We've already seen that Jesus had frequent interactions with the Pharisees, in which He confronted them, condemned some of their practices and their religious world view, but He also invited them to take part in God's eternal salvation.

We have also seen that in his dealings with the Pharisees, he addressed some of their theological views, which He tried to correct. In this chapter I want to investigate *how* Jesus reached out to the Pharisees. This might be an inspiration for Christians who want to reach out to religious Muslims with the Gospel. I want to emphasize that I am not limiting Jesus' approach to a method, or even worse 'the method', but Jesus' way of interacting with the Pharisees, can help us in our interactions with religious Muslims.

I want to summarize Jesus' interaction with the Pharisees in the word 'SAFT' (Arabic for 'good habit') which is an alliteration of:

- Socializing.
- Asking questioning.

- Finding common ground.
- Telling Stories.

## Socializing

*"That Pharisees share table fellowship with Jesus suggests that they do not consider his other associations to compromise their views or practices."*[86]

In the Gospel of Luke, we see Jesus frequently socializing with people of all strata of society. This particularly showed itself in the frequent meals He had with people. In fact, he was criticized by the Pharisees for sharing meals with people that they disapproved of. It seems that sharing meals was one of Jesus' favourite ways to socialize with people. In this way, He not only associated with sinners and tax-collectors, but also with the Pharisees! Jesus understood, as is common in many cultures today, that sharing meals with others is an important way to establish, deepen and enjoy intimate relationships with one another and to facilitate face-to-face conversations.

The Gospel of Luke we read of ten meals that Jesus shared with people, three of these were meals with Pharisees.[87] Jesus used these meals to establish closer relationships with the Pharisees and to speak to their hearts.

When we look at these three meals in more detail, we can observe the following:

- Although the motives for inviting Him might be questionable, Jesus didn't decline the invitation.
- Jesus association with the Pharisees socially, does not mean He agreed with all their actions or mindset.
- It was often during such meals that some of the key differences between Jesus and the Pharisees came to the front.[88]
- Jesus was an attentive observer of what took place around Him, and He addresses what He saw during His meal conversations.

---

86 Levine, Amy-Jill. *Luke's Pharisees*, chapter 4 in "In Quest of the Historical Pharisees" Neusner, Chilton, editors (Waco: Baylor University Press, 2007), 120.

87 Luke 7:36–50; Luke 11:37–54; Luke 14:1–24.

88 E.g. Jesus' identity and His authority to forgive sins; purity; table fellowship and the sabbath rules.

- In his conversations Jesus brought unto to the table what hitherto had been hidden in the thoughts of the Pharisees.

We can conclude that sharing a meal of delicacies provided Jesus with good opportunities to address delicate issues of the heart.

In our desire to have our religious Muslim friends see the beauty, the glory and attractiveness of Jesus, it is necessary that they see this in our own lives. How can they see Jesus in us when they don't know us? This means we need to associate with them and to share our lives with them and allow them to share their lives with us. No doubt, this includes sharing meals together.

## Asking Questions

We've seen that Jesus socialized with the Pharisees by accepting their invitations to share a meal with them. He used these opportunities not just for social chit-chat, but also to address key issues of the heart. One of the ways He did this was by *asking questions*.

Asking questions was a very common way for Jesus to communicate with people. The number of questions that Jesus asked as described in the New Testament runs into the hundreds.[89]

Also in his interactions with the Pharisees we find that Jesus frequently asked them questions, such as: *"Is it lawful to heal on the Sabbath or not?"(Luke 14:3)* and *"Why are you thinking these things in your heart? Which is easier: to say: 'Your sins are forgiven, or to say, 'Get up and walk?" (Matthew 9:5; Luke 5:23)* and *"John's Baptism was it from heaven or of human origin?"* (Luke 20: 4) and *"What do you think about the Messiah? Whose son is he?" (Matt. 22:41).*[90]

The questions Jesus asked the Pharisees often had to do with matters that related to the main conflicts that Jesus has with them, like theological issues

---

89 Bob Tiede lists 339 questions that Jesus asked: www.LeadingWithQuestions.com and Paul Weston calculated that Jesus asked 284 questions during evangelistic conversations; Paul Weston, "Evangelicals and Evangelism" in Not Evangelical Enough, ed. Iain Taylor (Carlyle: Paternoster, 2003).

90 Other examples are found in: Luke 6:9; Luke 14:5; Luke 20:4; Matt 12:34; Matt 15:3; Matt 23:17, 19; Luke 20:25.

about sabbath regulations, forgiveness of sins and His own identity. Sometimes it was part of his confronting them or condemning them or showing them His compassion. Sometimes the question came out of a story He told them.[91] Sometimes it was a way to refer them to their common ground.[92] Some were clearly rhetorical questions,[93] and others were 'counter questions' in response to questions He was asked by the Pharisees.[94]

In his E book *Now, that's a great question!*, Bob Tiede puts the questions Jesus asked in several categories, such as: questions that make a human connection; questions that cause introspection; questions to make an argument; warm-up questions; to the point questions; questions that reminded people of what they already knew; questions that asked for an opinion; questions that allowed people to voice their own need.[95]

In our interactions with religious Muslims, asking (and answering questions) will play an important role. Asking questions, will help us understand our Muslim friends better, deepen our relationships, open paths to deepen our conversation; enable us to reflect or learn to see things from another perspective. Our purpose of asking questions is not to embarrass our friend, or to set him or her up, but to genuinely understand, respect value and hear them. Our questions can cause introspection and encourage our Muslim friends to think more deeply about their faith and religious practices.

## Finding Common Ground

Jesus not only socialized with Pharisees and asked them questions, but He also looked for ways to build His teaching upon common ground.

The Pharisees considered themselves guardians of the Law of God as revealed in the Scriptures, including the Torah, the Psalms, the historical books, and the prophets. They wanted to obey these words as accurately as possible and to do so they needed to know how to implement them in their

---

91 Luke 7:41,42; Matt 21:31.

92 Luke 6:3; Luke 10:26; Matt 22:43–45.

93 Luke 11:18, 19; Luke 13:15, 16.

94 e.g. Luke 10:25,26.

95 Bob Tiede, *Now, that's a great question*!, pages 63–72 www.LeadingWithQuestions.com.

time. This meant they had created all sorts of extra traditions that would help them to obey the law to its minute details.

In His communication with the Pharisees Jesus sought to find common ground in their Scriptures, traditions, way of thinking and world view.

Jesus obviously knew ***their Scriptures.*** In fact, this was the main common ground between them. He regularly referred to the Old Testament with words such as: "Have you never read ...?"[96] He referred an expert of the law to the law.[97] He referred to OT people (e.g., Elijah, David, Jonah) and concepts and believes (e.g., Kingdom of God and angels) and He asked questions about their Scriptures. For example:

*"Why is it said that the Messiah is the son of David?" David himself declares in the Book of Psalms: 'The Lord said to my Lord: Sit at my right hand until I make your enemies a footstool for your feet.' David calls him 'Lord'. How then can he be his son?* (Luke 20:41–44)

Jesus not only was familiar with the Scriptures of the Pharisees; he also was familiar with their traditions. Because the Pharisees wanted to follow the law of God to its minute details, they had developed many additional rules that would help them obey the will of God in their daily life. Jesus shows He is familiar with these traditions and uses this as basis of his discussions with them.[98]

Thirdly, Jesus was familiar with their ***way of thinking, their worldview***. Even before they brought up a matter Jesus knew what was in their heart.[99] This insight might have been due to His prophetic insight, but also, we know He was a careful observer of people's habits and behaviour.[100]

In our dealing with religious Muslims, it is also important that we find common ground between their worldview and ours. We might find this in the Qur'an, and this should encourage us to be familiar with the content of the Qur'an. We might find common ground in their religious practices, such as prayer and fasting. We might find common ground in their daily live, in

---

96 E.g. Luke 6:3; Matthew 19:4; 21;16; 21:42.

97 Luke 10:25, 26.

98 Luke 12:37–52.

99 E.g. about forgiveness of sins, Luke 5:22ff; also Luke 7:39,40.

100 E.g. Luke 14:7; Luke 21:1,2.

which they seek to please God. We might find common ground in their concept of God, particularly when they refer to Him with ninety-nine names. We might find common ground in ethical or moral issues (such as abortion, euthanasia, homosexuality). No doubt, when we socialize with our religious Muslim friends and ask questions, we might discover more aspect of common ground. Of course, identifying common ground is important, but we should seek to move on. This brings us to the final element of Jesus' interaction with the Pharisees: telling stories.

## Telling stories

One of Jesus' most favourite ways to communicate the truth of God was by telling stories (parables) taken from daily lives, which presented a spiritual truth. Such a way of communication fits an honour/shame culture where indirect communication is considered very important so as not publicly shame people. Nevertheless, some of the stories have implicit condemnations.

In the Gospel of Luke Jesus speaks several parables that are explicitly directed to the Pharisees:

### *The parable of the money lender (Luke 7:36–50)*

While having a meal in the house of a Pharisee called Simon, Jesus tells 'the parable of the money lender'. This was in reference to a sinful woman who had been forgiven her sins and as a result had expressed great gratitude, while the Pharisee, who also was offered forgiveness didn't seem to have appreciated the offer as much.

### *Three parables about meals (Luke 14:1–23)*

During another meal with Pharisees and experts in the law, Jesus used three stories in which a meal featured, and this allowed Jesus to communicate spiritual truth about humility, self-righteousness and showing kindness and mercy.

### *Three parables about being lost and found (Luke 15:1–31)*

In response to the complaint of the Pharisees that Jesus ate with sinners, Jesus tells them three stories: the parable of the lost sheep, the parable of the lost coin and the parable of the lost son. The common theme of these three stories is the joy of the lost being found. In the parable of the lost son, the elder brother seems to reflect the attitude of the Pharisees, as I have pointed out earlier.

> The parables serve two main functions: 1) Jesus is defending his ministry to outcasts, and 2) he is implicitly asking the Pharisees and scribes to join the communal joy and celebration of the lost being found. The contrast between the behaviour of the Pharisees and scribes (15:2), and the rejoicing in heaven over the repentance of sinners (15:7, 10) is ominous. The Pharisees and scribes continue to reject God's plan.[101]

## *The parable of the Good Samaritan (Luke 10:25–37)*

Jesus spoke the parable of the Good Samaritan[102] in response to the question of an expert in the law. Although, the Pharisees are not mentioned, it is very likely that the law expert was a Pharisee.

> Although no Pharisee appears in the setting for the parable of the good Samaritan or the parable itself, Ringe proposes: "One might surmise from the question concerning eternal life that the lawyer is a Pharisee whose theology included belief in the resurrection of the dead ... The exchange of questions and answers that ensues fits what we know about the way various points of religious law were debated among the Pharisees, who were the principle forerunners of rabbinic Judaism."[103]

From other stories it is not explicitly said that Jesus addresses the Pharisees, but they thought he had them in mind.[104]

## *The parable of the Pharisee and the tax collector (Luke 18:9–13)*

One of Jesus' stories features a Pharisee as the main character of the story. The story is told 'to some who were confident of their own righteousness

---

[101] Gowler, 252.

[102] Luke 10:25–37.

[103] Levine, 121.

[104] For example, the parable of the shrewd manager (Luke 16:1–15) and the parable of the tenants (Luke 20:9–19).

and looked down on everyone else' (Luke 18:9). Although the Pharisees are not explicitly mentioned, it is obvious that they fit the description of those Jesus addresses with this story. The lesson that can be drawn from this parable is that God looks upon one's inner attitude of the heart more favourably then upon one's outward religious activities, such as tithing and fasting.

The story paints an accurate picture of many Pharisees and Jesus might have spoken it as a warning to them, to repent before it's too late. We know from later in the Bible that some Pharisees repented. Perhaps it was a story like this that was used by the Holy Spirit to lead them to conversion.

Sharing the truth of the Gospel with our religious Muslim friends, should not just be done by communicating with them propositional truths in a bare fashion, such as: God loves you; Christ died for our sins; Christ is risen; without being born again you cannot enter the Kingdom of God. It would be best to dress these and other propositional truths in a story.

"A propositional truth dedramatized has little to no communicative function."[105]

A Jewish teaching story goes like this

> Truth, naked and cold, had been turned away from every door in the village. Her nakedness frightened the people. When Parable found her, she was huddled in a corner, shivering and hungry. Taking pity on her, Parable gathered her up and took her home. There, she dressed Truth in story, warmed her and send her out again. Clothed in story, Truth knocked again at the villagers' doors and was readily welcomed into the people's houses. They invited her to eat at her table and warm herself at their fire.[106]

The Bible has provided us with hundreds of readymade 'dresses' the share truth with our religious Muslim friends, not only the parables of Jesus, but also stories from OT saints and prophets, and the people of Israel. Telling stories not only fits the cultural background of many of our Muslim friends, but stories also evoke emotion, draws in listeners, and speak metaphori-

---

[105] Callow, Kathleen. *Man and Message: A guide to meaning-based text analysis*, (University Press of America, 1998).

[106] Strauss, Robert. *Introducing Story-Strategic Methods*, (Eugene, Oregon: Wipf and Stock, 2017), 57.

cally. Let us follow Jesus' example as the Great Storyteller, to learn to share His story with our Muslim friends. We have learned that Jesus communicated with Pharisees through SAFT: socializing with them, asking them questions, finding common ground and telling them stories. As we have seen there are several close parallels between the Pharisees of Jesus' day and many religious Muslims of our time. Also, many of the Muslims we are relating with have grown up in cultures of honour and shame that are very similar to the culture and worldview of the Pharisees that Jesus related to. This should encourage us to explore using SAFT as a good habit in our dealing with our Muslim friends. Not as a method that guarantees 'success', but as a way takes the religious and cultural background into consideration when we desire to share our lives and, in this context, also the Gospel with our Muslim friends.

# CHAPTER 6
# GOD AT WORK AMONG THE PHARISEES – GAMALIEL, A PHARISAIC MAN OF PEACE?

*"But a **Pharisee** named Gamaliel, a teacher of the law, who was honoured by all the people, stood up in the Sanhedrin and ordered that the men be put outside for a little while."* (Acts 5:34; Acts 5:17–42

After the birth of the Church at Pentecost, the first believers faced many hardships and persecutions. Not surprisingly, many of their troubles were instigated by the Jewish religious leaders, among whom were the Pharisees. Nevertheless, God in His sovereignty, used one particular Pharisee, with the name Gamaliel, to protect the church leaders from harm.

We read in Acts 5 that Gamaliel was a teacher of the law, and very well respected. He speaks in favour of allowing the apostles to continue their preaching and work in Jesus' Name without hindrance from the Sanhedrin. Gamaliel does not urge repentance and faith in Jesus; he merely advocates that the Sanhedrin not interfere with the apostles. He couldn't decide for sure that this 'movement' was not of God.

He is considered a man of great authority. His orders are obeyed (Acts 5:34, 40) and his advice is heeded (Acts 5:40) In this way, the sentence of capital punishment was reduced to flogging (Acts 5:38–40).

There are good reasons to believe that Gamaliel was none other than Rabban (= our Rabbi in Aramaic) Gamaliel, the grandson of Hillel and that he served as the president of the Sanhédrin from 20 to 50. He was one of the most eminent tannaitic teachers of his generation. His grandfather, rabbi Hillel the Elder, had founded the most lenient version of Pharisaism. Gamaliel became Hillel's successor, leading the Pharisaic movement. He was one of the most respected, most influential Jew alive at that time.[107]

Although we don't read in the Bible that Gamaliel became a follower of Jesus, he is used by God to carry out His purposes.

---

[107] Abrami, Leo Michel. "Were all Pharisees Hypocrites?" *Journal of Ecumenical Studies, 47:3,* Summer 2012.

We also know that one of his bright students, by the name of Saul, became a strong follower of Jesus with the name Paul. Paul cites studying under Gamaliel as a prominent feature of his Jewish pedigree (Acts 22:3).

Gamaliel's argument for the Apostles in the Book of Acts has prompted numerous references to him as a covert Christian in order to help his fellow Christians. Some early manuscripts state that Gamaliel and his son Simeon were baptized by Peter and John.[108]

The Catholic Church recognizes Gamaliel as a saint. His remains are in the Christian Duomo in Pisa, Italy. The Early Church claimed Gamaliel in the August 3 celebration in the Roman Martyrology (300's) and a painting by a student of Carlo Saraceni, done in 1615 is called St. Stephen Mourned by Saints Gamaliel and Nicodemus and is in the Museum of Fine Arts in Boston.[109]

If not a believer, is might be argued that Gamaliel is a "Person of Peace" for the first Church.

In several church planting movements, the idea of finding a Person of Peace is one of the key principles.[110] The concept is taken from the instructions Jesus gave to his disciples when he sent them out in Matthew 10, Luke 9, and Luke 10. Jesus said:

> " Whatever town or village you enter, search there for some worthy person and stay at their house until you leave." (Matthew 10:11)

'Some worthy person' is referred to as 'a man of peace' in the Gospel of Luke.

> "When you enter a house, first say, 'Peace to this house.' If a man of peace is there, your peace will rest on him; if not, it will return to you. Stay in that house, eating and drinking whatever they give you, for

---

108 Clement, Recognitions, I, 65, in Alexander Roberts and James Donaldson, eds., The Ante-Nicene Fathers, the Writings of the Fathers down to A.D. 325, vol. 1 (Grand Rapids: Wm. B. Eerdmans, 1950).

109 Sandra Sweeny Silver, "Was Gamaliel a Christian?" https://earlychurchhistory.org/beliefs-2/was-gamaliel-a-christian/ (accessed March 18, 2021).

110 For example, the Disciple Making Movement (DMM). In their E-Book *Finding a Person of Peace*, DMMS Frontier Missions states: "Finding a Person of Peace is important in starting a Disciple-Making movement", page 3 and "Finding a Person of Peace is crucial starting a movement", 8.

> the worker deserves his wages. Do not move around from house to house." (Luke 10: 5, 6)

In the context of the commands of Jesus gave His disciples, these "people of peace" would be the residents who welcomed the travellers to their homes and extended hospitality for the entirety of their stay in that town. It is not clear from these passages whether these people accepted the message of the Gospel themselves. Although, it is not evident in the Scriptures that this principle was applied by the first church planters such as Paul, some suggest that the Ethiopian Eunuch, Cornelius, Lydia and the Philippian jailer are people of peace.[111]

DMMS Frontier Missions defines a person of peace as follows:

*A Person of Peace acts much like a doorway. They open the community to you and your message. They are a key influencers God has chosen. You work through them to reach the area.*[112]

Another definition of a person of peace:

*The Person of Peace is the one God has prepared to receive the Gospel into a community for the first time.*[113]

It is understood that such people of peace bring peace between the church planter and the community. They open the door to more people in the community hearing and being responsive to the message the visitors were bringing. A person of peace can be an influencer that becomes a catalyst to bridge the gospel into the community, irrespective of whether he or she themselves becomes a believer.

Whether Gamaliel fits all the descriptions of a person of peace is questionable, but in the year 33 before the Sanhedrin Gamaliel gave a reasonable, historically based argument that was used by God to prevent the deaths of the apostles. He promoted peace and as such helped the early Church to continue to grow.

---

111 Mumin Abdal Masih, "Beyond the Person of Peace" http://www.missionfrontiers.org/issue/article/beyond-the-person-of-peace (accessed March 18,2021).

112 Finding a Person of Peace, 3.

113 David Watson and Paul Watson, "Church Planting: Finding a Person of Peace" http://www.faithgateway.com/church-planting/#.WqpSQKZy6F4 (accessed March 18, 2021).

Perhaps in our desire to see Christ being glorified in the lives of our Muslim friends, God grants us a Muslim equivalent of Gamaliel, someone who is sympathetic to our cause, without necessarily being committed to it himself.

# CHAPTER 7
# GOD AT WORK AMONG THE PHARISEES – NICODEMUS: A SEARCHING PHARISEE

*"Now there was a Pharisee, a man named Nicodemus who was a member of the Jewish ruling council."* (John 3:1–21)

Although the Pharisees are sometimes seen as the most vehement antagonists of Jesus, it is obvious that not all Pharisees were like that. Some Pharisees have warned Jesus of evil attempts from Herod and several times Pharisees invited him to their dinners. We have also seen that some came to Jesus with questions, sometimes with wrong intents, but not always.

In the Gospel of John, we learn about Nicodemus, a Pharisee who came to Jesus with what seems a sincere and searching heart. That he had to come in the night might betray that he didn't feel secure to ask these questions in broad day light in front of his more opposing Pharisaic comrades, or perhaps, as was customary among Pharisees, to have a nightly discussion, to have some undisturbed time with Jesus to discuss matters of mutual interest.

Nicodemus considers Jesus a teacher come from God, but he had no perception of the real nature of Jesus. Jesus welcomes him without condemnation and carries on a conversation with him.

Nicodemus had not asked a question, but Jesus immediately begins to speak about the Kingdom of God and the necessity of re-birth. Did Jesus sense that Nicodemus' coming was predominantly to seek instruction in the way to eternal life?

The way to life for Nicodemus, like all good Pharisees, was the careful obedience to law of God. The idea of a rebirth had apparently not entered his mind. Nicodemus was familiar with the concept of the Kingdom of God; the eternal salvation and he most likely kept the law in order to enter into that Kingdom.

Jesus points him to the need for a rebirth in no uncertain terms. He basically tells him: "There is nothing we can accomplish to ensure entry into the

Kingdom of God. We need a re-birth. Such new birth can only be accomplished by the Spirit of God."[114] This must have been startling to Nicodemus as his response betrays. Jesus seems to be surprised about the lack of understanding on the part of Nicodemus. He points out that Nicodemus should have known that no one is able to enter the Kingdom in his own strength or righteousness.

Nicodemus, being a student and even a teacher of the Law of God, should have understood this. In answering his confusion, Jesus sends him back to the Scriptures. Jesus makes two references to the Old Testament, the Scriptures that Nicodemus must have been familiar with. He knew about the figure of 'the Son of Man' (Daniel 7:13,14) and of course he knew the story about 'the serpent lifted up' (Numbers 21:4–9). It is questionable whether he ever put the two references together in the way Jesus did.

The term 'Son of Man' was a clearly divine title and Jesus identifies Himself as this Son of Man. Jesus combines this with the story of the serpent of bronze that Moses had to make and put on a pole. Looking to 'the uplifted' serpent would provide healing and life. Jesus identified Himself (be it in somewhat indirect ways) with the brazen serpent. This 'lifting up' of the Son of Man most likely refers to His death on the cross but might also refer to His exaltation in majesty.

So when Nicodemus, a devout worshipper of the one true God, who was committed to live in obedience to the Law of God, came to Jesus to learn about the way to eternal life, Jesus took time for him, used Nicodemus' own words and Scriptures as a bridge to speak with him about the necessity of re-birth, made possible through the Holy Spirit, in lives of people who acknowledge that Jesus is the divine Son of Man who has to be lifted up for the salvation of the world.

> The new birth is the most 'extreme' of all doctrines, but it must be taught, especially to those who think of themselves as devout worshipers of God.[115]

We do not know how Nicodemus left the meeting with Jesus. Jesus let him go and did not pressurize him into accepting His teaching yet. Nevertheless,

---

[114] Barrs, Jerram. *Learning Evangelism from Jesus*, (Wheaton: Crossway, 2009), 207.

[115] Barr, *Learning Evangelism from Jesus*, 216.

Jesus' Word must have unsettled him and challenged His theology. It might have encouraged him to search the Scriptures even more and reflect more deeply about what Jesus said. At this point he is not ready to be a full disciple of Jesus, but brief comments about him later in the Gospel of John[116] seem to indicate that he has become a disciple of Jesus after all.

Jesus' conversion with Nicodemus can serve those who want to speak with religious Muslims about matters of eternal life. S.P. Steinhaus[117], suggests the 'Spirit-first method':

> Simply put, my approach is to focus initial discussion on the Holy Spirit thereby initially postponing discussion of the person of Jesus. By first discussing the Holy Spirit, I am able to get a hearing for the gospel and to reveal the source for meeting personal needs without being immediately rebuffed by standard Muslim objections. ... The Holy Spirit is the river of life that Jesus promised. He is the source, not only of spiritual power, but also to godly character. Freedom from anxiety, the ability to please God, increased spiritual devotion, the assurance of salvation, these are all blessings from the Spirit. And they are all things that many Muslims, both folk Muslims and Qur'anic Muslims, are seriously seeking and wanting today.[118]

Among our religious Muslim friends there might be those, who like Nicodemus want to explore deeper religious matters with us. May the Holy Spirit guide us to welcome them without reservations and take time with them to answer their questions with sensitivity, starting from familiar truth to unfamiliar truths. May God also give us patience to allow Him to continue to work in their lives, and not put any pressure on them.

---

[116] In John 7:50 Nicodemus defends Jesus in front of the chief priests and Pharisees; In John 19:3–40 we read that Nicodemus, together with Joseph of Arimathea, buried Jesus.

[117] A pseudonym of someone, who has been working among Muslims in SE Asia.

[118] S S.P. Steinhaus, "The Spirit-first Approach to Muslim Evangelism" *Review of Religious Research*, Vol. 47, No. 2 (Dec. 2005), pp. 162–174.

# CHAPTER 8
# GOD AT WORK AMONG THE PHARISEES – PAUL, A CONVERTED PHARISEE

Jesus' interaction with the Pharisees most likely was a matter of discussion within the Pharisaic community. After Jesus' death, resurrection and ascension to heaven, His followers, the apostles carried on His ministry in obedience to His commandment to "make disciples of all nations."(Matthew 28:19). In carrying out this ministry, they soon faced opposition, also from the Pharisees and they were warned to 'no longer speak in the name of Jesus' (Acts 5:27,28). Stephen, one of the followers of Jesus who carried on his public witness of Jesus, was stoned to death, by the members of the Jewish High Court (Sanhedrin). In the account of this stoning ceremony, we hear about a young man named Saul, at whose feet the people that stoned Stephen laid their coats. (Acts 7:58). We learn from the Bible that this Saul was a Pharisee, who had studied under Gamaliel, one of the most important and influential Pharisees of that time. (Acts 22:3). In his zealousness for God, Saul became one of the fiercest opponents of Christians. He was given authority to arrest and imprison followers of Jesus and even have them killed. His aggression was not limited to Christians living in Jerusalem or surrounding towns, but he even persecuted those abroad.

When he later speaks about this time of his life he says: *"I intensely persecuted the Church of God and tried to destroy it. I was advancing in Judaism beyond many of my own age among my people and was extremely zealous for the traditions of my fathers."* (Galatians 1:13,14)

Despite his religious zeal, he writes: *"I was once a blasphemer and a persecutor and a violent man."* (1 Tim. 1:13)

But God had His eye on this Pharisee, even from the time he was born (Galatians 1: 15) and had mercy on Saul. He revealed Himself to Saul through a vision (Acts 9), and used one of his disciples to bless and baptize him. This began a process of transformation in Saul's life, who now was called Paul. God used Paul to bring many people to believe in Jesus Christ and to plant many Churches throughout the Middle East. In God's providence His letters to the churches he planted have been incorporated into the Scriptures, the Word of God, through which He still speaks to His people to the present day.

Because Paul plays a prominent role in the New Testament we know quite a bit about him, which is relevant for our topic on Jesus and the Pharisees in relation to sharing the Gospel with religious Muslims.

## Was Paul still a Pharisee?

After Paul met with the risen Christ in a vision, his life was radically transformed. He was still zealous for God, but now not to as a means to salvation, but as a consequence of being saved through his faith in Jesus Christ. He travelled to several places, including Greece, Macedonia, and present-day Turkey. His ministry not only resulted in many new churches being planted, but he also faced fierce opposition. Several times he was put on public trial and was asked to justify was he was doing. During one of these trials, before the Sanhedrin, the Jewish High Court, that was made up of both Sadducees and Pharisees, he said:

*"My brothers, I am a Pharisee, descended from Pharisees, I stand on trial because of the hope of the resurrection of the dead."* (Acts 23:6).

He identified with the Pharisees and mentioned one of their key doctrines that distinguished them from the Sadducees, namely that human beings are raised from the dead.

What is remarkable here is that more than twenty years after his miraculous conversion on the road to Damascus, Paul still claims to be a Pharisee with Pharisaic heritage. As we will see, it is unlikely he was a Pharisee in all aspects, but here he points out that he agrees with an important part of the Pharisaic theology, namely the resurrection of the death.

> To be sure, the Pharisaic and Christian understandings of the law were very different, and to this extent Paul could not have claimed to be a Pharisee ... however Paul, even as a Christian, was still in many ways a Pharisee.[119]

Paul did not see a contradiction between a key doctrine of Pharisaism and a key doctrine of the Christian faith, in fact, he seems to imply that the resurrection of Christ is a confirmation of the doctrine of the Pharisees about life after death.

---

[119] Howard Marshall, I. *Acts,* Tyndale New Testamant Commentaries (Grand Rapids: Wm. B. Eerdmans, 1980), 365.

> What Paul was now in effect claiming was that one could be a Christian, while accepting the Pharisaic point of view, or more precisely, that Pharisaic Judaism found its fulfillment in Christianity.[120]

> Paul declared solidarity with the Pharisees and with their hope in the resurrection of the dead. ... Pauls' statement is an affirmation that there is a continuity between Judaism (Pharisaism) and Christianity that cannot be denied; the hope of the resurrection serves as the common ground.[121]

This incident seems to indicate that the resurrection of the dead could be considered common ground between Pharisaism and Christianity.

As a result of Paul's comments, we read that some Pharisees responded that they didn't find anything wrong in Paul and suggested that an angel or a spirit might have spoken to him and have given him the insight that he expounded.

> Some of the teachers of the law, who were Pharisees are open to Paul's revelation. They are upon the threshold of Christianity, but they do not cross that line of belief. They suggest that some type of revelation to Paul was possible, but do not admit that the resurrected Jesus could have appeared to him. ... They hover near Christianity, but never take that final, all-important step: they do not believe in Jesus the resurrected Lord. The hope of the resurrection is the closest link between Pharisaism and Christianity, but in this scene Paul is the only Pharisee who sees that hope fulfilled in Jesus of Nazareth. Paul is the true Pharisee ..."[122]

During a later trial, before king Agrippa, Paul again gives a clear account of his convictions and what had caused his transformation. He said:

*"The Jewish people all know the way I have lived ever since I was a child, from the beginning of my life in my own country, and also in Jerusalem. They have known me for a long time and can testify, if they are willing, that I conformed to the strictest sect of our religion, living as a Pharisee. And now it is because of my hope in what God has promised our ancestors that I am on*

---

[120] Ibid. 364.

[121] Gowler, 289.

[122] Ibid. 290, 291.

*trial today. This is the promise our twelve tribes are hoping to see fulfilled as they earnestly save God day and night. King Agrippa, it is because of this hope that these Jews are accusing me."* (Acts 26:4–7)

Paul again clearly associates with the Pharisees. Again, as we saw before, he links his present convictions to the beliefs of the Pharisees. He has come to see that the resurrection of Christ is indeed the fulfilment of the hope that he and his Pharisaic forefathers were eagerly anticipating.

> This narrative reinforces that Christianity is the logical and legitimate outgrowth of Pharisaism ... All Jews, Paul says, have hope for the future resurrection. But in addition to this future hope, Paul offers them a present reality: the resurrection of Jesus. Some Pharisees, and Paul is the prime example, have accepted that present reality. Other Pharisees, – indeed most Pharisees – have not.[123]

From the above incidents in Paul's life, we learn that although he was now a follower of Jesus Christ, he still considered himself a Pharisee, and testified that Christ is the ultimate fulfilment of the deepest desires of the Pharisees, namely the hope of eternal salvation in the presence of the living God.

The realization that even the Apostle Paul twenty years after his conversion still considers himself in some way a Pharisee, may suggest that Muslims that have come to follow Christ could still refer to themselves as Muslim followers of Jesus, as the Insider Movement suggests. This is a topic that has stirred up much discussion among Christian missiologists and is beyond the scope of this document.

But, while Christ was indeed the fulfilment of the hope of the Pharisees, many of them did not become followers of Christ and the reason for this we might learn from Paul himself when he describes his transformation in one of his letters, to which we now turn.

### Reorientation of Pharisaic teaching and practices

Although Paul, as we have seen, considered himself still a Pharisee, particularly because of their key doctrine of life after death, this doesn't mean that he considered all his former convictions as being fulfilled in Christ. Some could no longer be part of his life and has to be thrown out, like garbage.

---

[123] Ibid. 295, 296.

This process of sifting what to continue and what to throw out, seems to have been referred to by Jesus when He said:

*"Therefore every teacher of the law who has become a disciple of the kingdom of heaven is like the owner of a house who brings out of his storeroom new treasures as well as old."* (Matthew 13:52)

Paul describes this process of sifting clearly in his letter to the church of Philippi, particularly in chapter 3:1–14. One of the Pharisaic doctrines Paul had come to radically disagree with was the place of the law of God in attaining righteousness. He writes:

*If someone else thinks they have reasons to put confidence in the flesh, I have more: circumcised on the eight day ... in regard to the law, a Pharisee ... as for righteousness based on the law, faultless. But whatever were gains to me I now consider loss for the sake of Christ. What is more, I consider everything a loss because of the surpassing worth of knowing Christ Jesus my Lord, for whose sake I have lost all things. I consider them garbage, that I may gain Christ and be found in him, not having a righteousness that comes from the law, but that which is through faith in Christs – the righteousness that comes from God on the basis of faith.* (Phil. 3:3–9)

Before his conversion Paul was a religious man, who lived his life as much as possible in agreement with the law of God. In the eyes of man, maybe even in his own eyes, he was faultless. It seems that if someone would be entitled to enter paradise on the basis of his behaviour it would be Paul, or rather Saul, as he was still called then. But once He saw the richness of Jesus Christ, he began to see that what he considered as spiritually valuable, was in fact garbage compared to what God had given him when he came to faith in Jesus Christ.

> Like most "religious" people today, Paul had enough morality to keep him out of trouble, but not enough righteousness to get him into heaven! It was not bad things that kept Paul away from Jesus—it was good things! He had to lose his "religion" to find salvation.[124]

---

124 Wiersbe, W. The *Bible Exposition Commentary, New Testament, volume* 2 (Colorado Springs: Cooks Communications Ministries, 1989), 84r.

As a Pharisee, Paul was brought up with a high respect for the law of God. He considered the law of God (as found in the Torah) the ultimate expression of the righteousness of God. It showed mankind God's standard for purity, perfection, holiness, and justice. He had learned to keep the law as well as he could. He believed that gradually with his own power he would be mastering the ability to keep the law and in doing so become righteous in the eyes of God. But he had come to see that this is a futile attempt. It would not only wear him out, but also would make him bitter, judgement and joyless. When he learned about Jesus Christ, he began to see that all that he had attempted to get by keeping the law, would be given to him, graciously by God, due to His faith in Jesus Christ. The righteousness he tried to attain by self-effort, was given to him as a grace-gift. Paul is not denouncing the law of God, nor the righteousness it demanded. But now he is denouncing the confidence that his own good deeds, religious efforts, law-keeping, self-improvement can make someone right with God. Once he considered these precious things he boasted in, but now, after he has come in relationship with Jesus Christ, he has found such a spiritual wealth that he puts he former religious valuables out of his life as rubbish.

The radical transformation from boasting in the Law of God to boasting in Jesus Christ is something that God not only did in Saul, but He is anxious to do in the lives of our Muslim friends.

# CHAPTER 9
# GOD AT WORK AMONG THE PHARISEES – PHARISAIC CHRISTIANS: NEED FOR CONTINUING DISCIPLESHIP

*... some of the believers who belonged to the party of the* ***Pharisees*** *...*
(Acts 15:1–22)

After the Spirit had descended upon the Church, the number of believers began to grow rapidly. After Peter's sermon on Pentecost about 3000 people were baptized (Acts 2:41) and the number of disciples of Jesus kept increasing rapidly and a large number of priests became obedient to the Christian faith. (Acts 6:1, 7). Also, Pharisees had been converted. We don't know their number or how this conversion took place, but we read in Acts 15 about believers *who belonged to the party of the Pharisees*. They are referred to as believers and there is nothing in the text to suggest that they had not fully given their lives to Jesus and acknowledged Him as their Lord and Saviour.

Nevertheless, it seems that their legalism had not totally left them yet. This particularly came up in the discussion about how non-Jewish believers can join the Christian community. Apparently they were still championing the importance of the law, saying: "The Gentiles must be circumcised and required to keep the law of Moses." (Acts 15:5)

This conviction was still quite strong in the early church, particularly in the church in Jerusalem and other Jewish contexts. When Peter had a meal in the house of Cornelius we read: "The *circumcised believers* criticized him and said "You went into the house of uncircumcised men and ate with them." (Acts 11:3)

Of course most of the first believers were from Jewish background and most likely were circumcised believers. We don't know whether these people where the same as those who belonged to the party of the Pharisees and spoke at the Council. In Acts 15:1 we read: "Certain people came down from Judea to Antioch and were teaching the believers: "Unless you are circumcised, according to the custom taught by Moses, you cannot be saved."

These were influential people of the Jewish church, who also had the capacity to teach. Paul and Barnabas strongly disagreed with them (Acts 15:2) and that is the reason why the meeting of the global church leaders had to take place.

During that important first Church council meeting, the believers of the party of the Pharisees, spoke up first and repeated the words of the teachers in Antioch. This seems to imply that those people who had gone to Antioch were believers of Pharisaic background, or at the least very sympathetic towards their convictions.

So, we know there were converted Pharisees in the Church. They had given their life to Jesus. They must have acknowledged Him as Lord and Saviour. But old habits seem to die hard.

> We probably underestimate what a colossal step it was for dyed-in-the wool Jewish legalists to adopt a new way of thinking.[125]

In Galatians 2:11–19 Paul speaks of believers who belonged to the 'circumcision group' (vs 12), who influenced Peter and Barnabas. These might have been the same converted Pharisees.

These people are often referred to as 'Judaizers', who are defined as:

> A group in the primitive Church who sought to overlay the simple ordinances of Christianity with Judaic observances and rites.[126]

It is obvious that the transition from Judaism to Christianity could hardly be made without difficulty.

> To the Jew it must have seemed almost incredible that he should divest himself of the observance of Mosaic Law, and equally incredible that the Gentile should be admitted into the Kingdom of God without accepting the same Law. It was inevitable that the question should soon arise in the early days of the Church, whether the Church of the future should be Catholic or Jewish. It was only to be expected that this controversy should give rise to a party in the Church who were in favor of the latter alternative, consisting of those who, being Christians, yet

---

125 Howard Marshall, 249.

126 https://www.studylight.org/encyclopedias/nut/j/judaizers.html (accessed March 18, 2021).

> retained their affection for the Mosaic Law and wished to impose it upon every member of the Christian Church. On the other hand, the keen intellect of a Stephen or a Paul saw at once that any attempt to enforce the Mosaic Law or even the initiatory rite of circumcision upon the Gentiles, meant stagnation and death to the Church.[127]

Although, I don't think ***all*** Judaizers were converted Pharisees, it is very likely that most converted Pharisees were Judaizers.

> The words of the Pharisees in Acts 15:5 … closely parallel many of the words and actions of the Pharisees in the Gospel of Luke (e.g. Luke 5:30, 33; 6:2, 7; 11:38–42; 14:1–6; 15:2; 18:12) The Gospel's Pharisees are usually concerned about Jesus' actions that are contrary to their interpretation of the law. In a similar way, these Pharisees are concerned that Gentiles have to be circumcised and have to obey the law … Pharisaic legalists were rebuked by Jesus, and their position is also rejected here.[128]

The Council of Jerusalem addressed the subject brought up by the believers who belonged to the party of the Pharisees, namely whether the believers from Gentile background must be circumcised keep the law of Moses in order to be part of the Church.

> The debate in Acts 15 is reminiscent of the debates Jesus had with the Pharisees concerning purity regulations. Jesus had focused the debate upon the general social purpose of purity rules and declared that God was open to all persons.[129]

After much discussion, four leaders spoke to address this issue. Firstly, Peter speaks about his interaction with the Gentile Cornelius. He had learned that both Jew and Gentile are saved by the grace of the Lord Jesus. God had accepted them based on their faith and purified their heart through faith in Jesus and there was no need to put the yoke of the law on them (Acts 15:7–12).

---

127 https://www.studylight.org/dictionaries/hdn/j/judaizing.html (accessed March 18, 2021).

128 Gowler,282.

129 Ibid, 285.

Secondly, Paul and Barnabas testified about the signs and wonders that God has done among Gentiles, showing His love and acceptance, without the law and circumcision. (15:12).

Thirdly, James confirms the words of the previous speakers, by referring to the words found in Amos 9:11,12, where God promises that He would look favourably upon mankind who would seek Him. Amos also spoke about Gentiles who bear the name of the Lord. (Acts 15:13–18)

So those present agreed that the believers from Gentile background should not be required to be circumcised and to keep the law of Moses in order to be part of the Church.

James, who seems to have been the senior leader of the church in Jerusalem, concluded the meeting with a strong statement:

> It is my judgment, therefore, that we should not make it difficult for the Gentiles who are turning to God. Instead we should write to them, telling them to abstain from food polluted by idols, from sexual immorality, from the meat of strangled animals and from blood." (Acts 15:19–21)

A welcome letter was written by the apostles and elders to the Gentile believers in Antioch, which was received with great joy.

The Pharisaic Christians' position was rejected, the unity of the church was restored. The Pharisaic Christians, it seems, are included in 'the whole church' (15:22)

Although the unity of the church was restored, it seems that the ideas of the Judaizers did not totally disappear.

When we read the book of Acts and the letters written by Paul carefully, we regularly find references to the attempts of 'the Judaizers' to gain their end, and of the resolute resistance to them of by Paul and others.[130]

Some commentators believe that the zealous Jews mentioned in Acts 21:20 were actually Christian Pharisees. "You see, brother, how many thousands of Jews have believed, and all of them are zealous for the law."

---

[130] Galatians 2; 2 Corinthians 11; Philippians 3.

The ideas verbalized at the Council of Jerusalem by 'the believers who belonged to the party of the Pharisees' seems to have continued and threatened the purity of the Gospel. It seems that Paul's letter to the churches in Galatia, was particularly written with the Judaizes in mind:

> ... the occasion which prompted Paul to write this letter was the sinister and, to some extent successful influence which Judaistic troublemakers were exerting upon the churches ... And the purpose was to counteract this dangerous error by re-emphasizing the glorious gospel of free grace in Christ Jesus ...[131]

What becomes clear is that some Pharisees had come to believe that Jesus is the Messiah, had professed faith in Him, had become members of the church, yet retained many of their pharisaic tenets. They continued to be zealous for the law and sought to supplement Paul's gospel by requiring that the basics of the Law be followed: circumcision and food laws. Although at the Council of Jerusalem, their convictions were proven wrong, by Peter and James, it seems that Paul in particular addresses their opinions most strongly and most clearly. After all, being a converted Pharisee himself, he knew their mindset. Particularly in his letter to the Galatians, he counteracts the error of the Pharisaic Christians and other Judaizers most clearly. He pointed out that they perverted the Gospel of grace and threatened the freedom believers have in Christ.

The presence of the converted Pharisees in the church and their influence, should remind us that when someone comes to faith in Christ, although he or she is born anew, his or her former way of life and thinking and worldview is not immediately totally renewed.

It is important to keep this in mind when Muslims come to faith in Jesus. Those that were raised as a Pharisee did not immediately lose their Pharisaic way of thinking. Those that are raised as a Muslim do not immediately lose their Islamic way of thinking.

I once heard someone say: "It is easier to take someone out of Islam, than to take Islam out of someone." Renewing one's mind and thinking is a process that takes time. The Holy Spirit starts this renewing process at someone's

---

[131] Hendriksen, William. *Galatians,* New Testament Commentary, (Edinburgh: The Banner of Truth Trust, 1969), 21.

conversion and will continue hammering, polishing, kneading until Jesus becomes more visible and His glory shines through more brightly.

In his book *the Islamic Jesus*, Mustafa Akyol, argues there is a link between the Judaizers of Paul's time and the Muslims of our present day.

> Here is a paradox of world-historical proportions: Jewish Christianity indeed disappeared within the Christian church, but was preserved in Islam.[132]

Although, many people will not agree with this hypothesis, nevertheless, it is clear that there are parallels between Pharisees of Jesus' and Paul's day, as has been pointed already.

When we can learn from the presence of believers, who belonged to the party of the Pharisees in the early Church, and the discussions they caused, is the need for ongoing discipleship of Christians of Muslim background and also the need of patience to see them grow into full maturity. Perhaps in light of the above, Paul's letter to the Galatians, who had come under the influence of the thinking of people like the converted Pharisees of Acts 15, is an important tool to help our brothers and sisters from Muslim background mature in Christ.

---

[132] Akyol opens his chapter 4 entitled 'The missing link' (referring to the missing link between Jewish Christianity and Islam) with this quote from Hans-Joachim Schoeps, religious historian and philosopher, 81.

# CHAPTER 10
# CHRIST, THE CULMINATION OF THE LAW (ROMANS 10:1–15)

*"Christ is the culmination of the law so that there may be righteousness for everyone who believes."* (Romans 10:4)

In Romans 10:1–15 Paul writes passionately about religious Jews. The words he uses to describe them can be applied to religious Muslims of our day. In this final chapter I want to highlight several aspects to encourage us in our relationship with our religious Muslim friends.

## Zealous for God

Paul refers to the religious Jews, including the Pharisees, of his day as being 'zealous for God.' This zeal expressed itself in keeping the religious duties, in observing the law to its details, in maintaining purity. Paul himself referred to his zeal as a Pharisee. In his life, it expressed itself in persecuting the church (Phil. 2:6), in holding on to the traditions (Gal. 1:14).

Also, among religious Muslims of our day we observe a zealousness. Sometimes it is seen in their using violence to protect the honour of their religion, but most often it is seen in a commitment to their religious duties, such as prayer and fasting. Unfortunately, religious zealousness can often be more a hindrance, rather than a help in our relationship with God.

## They lacked enlightened knowledge

Zeal can hide an absence of knowledge. Of course, the religious Jews had certain knowledge, they knew certain religious facts. They might even have learned (like many religious Muslims of our time) parts of God's Word by heart. They may have had academic knowledge, knowledge of the head, but they lacked spiritual knowledge, a knowledge of the heart. And because of this, they missed the point.

## They did not know the righteousness of God

Paul specifies what he means by his statement that the zealous, religious Jews lacked enlightened knowledge, namely that they did not know the righteousness of God.

Even though they knew the law of God and were zealous to follow *its letter*, they seemed to have missed *the spirit* of God's law. In His law, God had revealed His character, His love, His holiness, His desire for relationship and communion with His people. He had revealed His standard of behaviour and had provided for ways to restore a broken relationship with Himself, through the sacrificial system He gave them.

The zealous, religious Jews knew that God was righteous, and that His law was an expression of His righteousness. But they did not 'see' that God's demand for righteousness is a gift that He eagerly wants to give to His people.

## They sought to establish their own righteousness

The Jews that Paul writes about knew that God was righteous, but they failed to see that mankind is unable to live up to God's righteous standards, as expressed in the law and that God doesn't demand this of us.

They wanted to present to God their religious zeal to attain His righteousness by doing good works but alas, this is a dead-end street. Mankind is never able to fulfil God's righteousness, despite their good intentions and their religious zeal. The religious Jews, like the religious Muslims of our day, established their own standards of what is right and wrong, which they thought were based on the law of God and therefore must be acceptable by God. But alas, they were mistaken.

## They did not submit to God's righteousness

The tragic consequence of seeking to establish one's own righteousness, or to put it differently, to create one's own road to God and His eternal presence, is that men not only are blind for the road that God has built for everyone, but that one opposes the idea that such a road actually exists.

How tragic that religious zeal, doing good in name of God, even religious duties such as prayer, fasting, pilgrimage, almsgiving that is done in order to attain the righteousness that God demands, becomes one of the biggest obstacles to receive what it aims for. The reason? Righteousness is mistakenly considered a reward for things done, instead of a gift, graciously provided for by the Holy, Righteous and Forgiving God.

**Christ is the culmination of the Law**

The law of God, with its perfect standards of conduct, was a good expression of the character of God. It was given by God to mankind to make clear who God is and what He demands of man. But mankind is not able to do what the law requires. The sooner one acknowledges this the better. They who do not acknowledge this, seek to please God with their religious deeds and they discover this is useless. No one can establish his own righteousness in the sight of God.

Christ is the culmination of the law so that there may be righteousness for everyone who believes.

> In our text, Paul is explaining why some very religious people missed salvation. The Jews were about as religious as anyone could be. They were fastidious about keeping the Law of Moses. In fact, to interpret that Law correctly, so that nobody missed it, they devised hundreds of extra laws. Keeping the Sabbath holy wasn't specific enough for them, so they had rules about how far you could walk and about what constituted work on the Sabbath. ... They had rules on washing and cleanliness that added to the Law (Mark 7:3). But they missed salvation and even crucified the Saviour!
>
> Religious people miss salvation because they think that their good works will satisfy God's demand for righteousness, so they don't trust in Christ for righteousness ... Sometimes we see people who are atheists or blatantly anti-Christian and we think, "They will never come to faith in Christ!" But then we see good, nice, religious people and think, "They don't need to come to Christ." Wrong on both counts! ... But the religious Pharisees were not good enough to get into heaven by their religiosity. They needed the new birth if they wanted to see the kingdom of God (John 3:3).[133]

---

[133] Steve Cole, *Why Religious People Miss Salvation* Romans 10:1–4, quoted on https://www.preceptaustin.org/romans_101-4, (accessed March 18, 2021).

Once we begin to understand the tragic condition that our religious Muslim friends are in, namely that in their eagerness to be acceptable by God, they are so focused on their religious duties and seek to perform these in a right manner and a zeal that looks very impressive, that they are unable and unwilling to receive God's gift of righteousness in the person of Jesus Christ. Or to put it differently: their hands are full of 'presents' they want to offer to God to show Him they love, respect, and obey Him that they cannot receive the gracious, loving gift of God's forgiveness, acceptance, eternal salvation, because Christ has fulfilled God's law on their behalf. How tragic!

This condition of our Muslim friends should fill our hearts with anguish and concern. How is it possible that they seem to be so close to God's precious gift of receiving His righteousness which means eternal salvation, and at the same time are so far away?

Our compassion should then express itself in similar ways as it did Paul for his religious countrymen, namely in fervent prayer and willing feet.

### Fervent prayer

One of the best ways we can serve our Muslim friends is to pray to God on their behalf, often and specific. We can pray for all aspect of their live. We can pray that God will open their eyes to see the impossibility of establishing their own righteousness. We can pray that during their times of prayer God will speak to them. We can pray that their desire for doing good, but their inability to live up to their own desired standards will create the same sentiment that Paul expressed in Romans 7:21–25: *"So I find this law at work: Although I want to do good, evil is right with me. For in my inner being I delight in God's law; but I see another law at work in me, waging war against the law of my mind and making me a prisoner of the law of sin at work within me. What a wretched man I am! Who will rescue me from this body that is subject to death? Thanks be to God, who delivers me through Jesus Christ our Lord!"*

We can pray that God will speak to them through a dream and stir up their heart to bow their knee before Jesus Christ and call upon the name of the Lord in order to be saved, for "everyone who call on the name of the Lord will be saved." (Romans 10:13, Joel 2:32)

## Willing feet

It is our responsibility as followers of Jesus, to come alongside our Muslim friends. We, whose eyes have already been opened to see the glory of Jesus Christ, should not be proud or judgmental, but help fellow seekers after God to draw closer to God's written and incarnated Word. We need to share our lives with our Muslim friends and show them what it means that Christ is the culmination of the law. Sharing our lives with them, gives us opportunities to speak the truth of God as we have come to understand it. May we be wise in the way we act towards our Muslim friends, making the most of every opportunity and may our conversations with them be always full of grace, seasoned with salt, so that we know how to answer everyone (based on Colossians 4:5,6).

May God grant that our Muslim friends, many of whom, might be like the Pharisees of Jesus' day, begin to seek after truth and meet with Jesus in the night, like Nicodemus; or meet with the risen Christ, while zealously pursuing their religious goals and be transformed like Saul. May God grant that many of them will part of the Church of Jesus Christ, as many of the Pharisees did in the early church.

May, ultimately, all our Muslim friends come to understand that Christ is the culmination of the law and heed the words of Christ:

*Come to me, all you who are weary and burned, and I will give you rest. Take my yoke upon you and learn from me, for I am gentle and humble in heart, and you will find rest for your souls. For my yoke is easy and my burden is light.* (Matthew 11:28–30)

# BIBLIOGRAPHY

Abrami, Leo Michel. "Were all Pharisees Hypocrites?" *Journal of Ecumenical Studies,* 47:3, Summer 2012

Akyol, Mustafa. *The Islamic Jesus: How the King of the Jews Became a Prophet of the Muslims*, (New York: St. Martins Press, 2017)

Barrs, Jerram. *Learning Evangelism from Jesus*, (Wheaton: Crossway, 2009)

Benson, Joseph. *Commentary of the Old and New Testaments* (New York: T. Carlton & J. Porter, 1857)

Bickerman, Elias. The Maccabees, (New York: Schocken Books, 1947)

Blomberg, Craig L. *Contagious Holiness: Jesus' meals with sinners*, (Westmont, Illinois: InterVarsity Press, 2005)

Callow, Kathleen. *Man and Message: A guide to meaning-based text analysis*, (Lanham: University Press of America, 1998).

Gowler, David B. *Portraits of the Pharisees in Luke and Acts*, (New York: Peter Lang, 1991)

Hovestol Tom. *Extreme Righteousness*, (Milton Keyes: Authentic Media Limited, 2013)

Davies, W.D. *Introduction to Pharisaism*, (Minneapolis: Fortress Press, 1954)

Eckstein, Yehiel. *What Christians Should Know About Jews and Judaism*. (Waco: Word Books, 1984)

Farooq, Mohammad Omar. *Toward our Reformation: From Legalism to Value-Oriented Islamic Law and Jurisprudence,* (London: The International Institute of Islamic Thought, 2012)

Finkel, Asher. *The Pharisees and the Teacher of Nazareth* (Leiden: E.J. Brill, 1964)

Hendriksen, William. *Galatians,* New Testament Commentary, (Edinburgh: The Banner of Truth Trust, 1969)

Howard Marshall, I. *Acts,* Tyndale New Testament Commentaries (Grand Rapids: Wm. B. Eerdmans, 1980)

Johnson, Paul. *A History of The Jews* (London: Weidenfeld & Nicolson, 1987)

Karcic, Fikret. *The Other European Muslims: A Bosnian Experience* (Sarajevo: Center for Advanced Studies, 2015)

Ladd, George Eldon. *A Theology of the New Testament* (Grand Rapids: Wm. B. Eerdmans, 1959)

Levine, Amy-Jill. *Luke's Pharisees*, chapter 4 in "In Quest of the Historical Pharisees" Neusner, Chilton, editors (Waco: Baylor University Press, 2007)

MacDonald, William. *Believer's Bible Commentary* (Nashville: Thomas Nelson, 2016)

M. Numan Malkoc and Peter Pikkert. *A Comparative Dictionary of Religious Terms in Islam and Christianity.* (Ancaster: ALEV Books, 2020).

Morris, Leon. *Luke,* The Tyndale NT Commentaries, (Grand Rapids: Wm. B. Eerdmans, 1974)

Polhill, John. *Paul and his letters* (Nashville: B&H Academic, 1999).

Ramadan, Tariq. *Western Muslims and the Future of Islam* (Oxford: Oxford University Press, 2005)

Schürer, Emile. *The History of the Jewish People in the Age of Christ, Volume 2*; (Edinburgh: Bloomsbury Publishing PLC)

S.P. Steinhaus, "The Spirit-first Approach to Muslim Evangelism" *Review of Religious Research*, Vol. 47, No. 2 (Dec. 2005), pp. 162–174.

Strauss, Robert. *Introducing Story-Strategic Methods*, (Eugene, Oregon: Wipf and Stock, 2017).

Travers Herford, Robert. *The Pharisees*, (Basingstoke: MacMillan, 1924).

Varner, William C. "Jesus and the Pharisees: A Jewish Perspective", *The Quarterly Journal*; The Newsletter Publication of Personal Freedom Outreach 16, no 3 (July–September 1996).

Weston, Paul. "Evangelicals and Evangelism" in Not Evangelical Enough, ed. Iain Taylor (Carlyle: Paternoster, 2003).

Wiersbe, W. *The Bible Exposition Commentary*, New Testament, volume 2 (Colorado Springs: Cooks Communications Ministries, 1989).

Wright, N.T. *The New Testament and the People of God* (Minneapolis: Fortress Press, 1992).

Young, Brad H. Jesus, the Jewish Theologian. (Grand Rapids, Michigan: Baker Publishing Group, 1993).

**Bert de Ruiter**

# Sharing Lives

## Overcoming Our Fear of Islam

Many European Christians fear that Europe will gradually turn into Eurabia, or Islamic domination of Europe, and they ignore the efforts of Muslims to adapt to the European context, a situation pointing to a future scenario of Euro-Islam, or Islam being Europeanized. The author argues that instead of an attitude of fear, which leads to exclusion, Christians should develop an attitude of grace, which leads to embrace.

The author developed a short course to help Christians overcome their fear of Islam and Muslims and to encourage Christians to share their lives with Muslims and to share the truth of the Gospel.

Pb. • pp. XIII + 209 • £ 13.95 • $ 22.95 • € 14.90
ISBN 978-3-941750-22-7

# Sharing Lives

## Course book

A course to help Christians share their lives with Muslims

Available in
**English** (978-3-95776-202-3), **Africaans** (978-3-95776-205-4), **Dutch** (978-3-95776-203-0), **Finnish** (978-3-95776-209-2), **French** (978-3-95776-208-5), **German** (978-3-95776-201-6), **Hungarian** (978-3-95776-204-7), **Italian** (978-3-95776-206-1), **Portuguese** (978-3-95776-210-8), **Romanian** (978-3-95776-211-5), **Russian** (978-3-95776-212-2) and **Spanish** (978-3-95776-207-8).

Pb. • ca. 80 pp. • £ 7.50 • $ 12.00 • € 9.50

www.ingramcontent.com/pod-product-compliance
Ingram Content Group UK Ltd.
Pitfield, Milton Keynes, MK11 3LW, UK
UKHW021654190726
13853UKWH00001B/246